Can Modernity Survive?

Can Modernity Survive?

Agnes Heller

University of California Press
Berkeley   Los Angeles

University of California Press
Berkeley and Los Angeles, California

© 1990 by Agnes Heller

ISBN 0–520–07254–5

Library of Congress Cataloging-in-Publication Data

Heller, Agnes,
  Can modernity survive? / Agnes Heller.
    p.   cm.
  Includes index.
  ISBN 0–520–07254–5
  1. Postmodernism—Social aspects.   2. Civilization, Modern—20th
century.   I. Title.
HM73H38 1990
303.4—dc20   90-10996
                                                                                   CIP

Printed in Great Britain

Contents

Acknowledgements

With the exception of Chapter 5, all the essays collected in this volume are altered or reworked versions of papers first delivered as lectures. Questions, critical remarks and debates following those lectures gave me new food for thought. I owe thanks to all those who provided me with the opportunity to try out my ideas – my colleagues and the students of the New School for Social Research, of the University of Notre Dame, of the University of Frankfurt, of Monash University (Melbourne), of Rutgers University, of the Cardozo School of Law, and to all the participants at the East/West Philosophy Conference at the University of Honolulu.

I thank my research assistant, Wayne Klein, for his conscientious editorial work and for preparing the index.

I conducted many a passionate discussion with Ferenc Fehér about just about everything written in this book. His stubborn resistance to accept some of my theoretical escapades made me rethink a few issues more than once, and to rewrite Chapter 5 twice. This is one way to thank him for being angry.

Agnes Heller
New York

Introduction

I

Having finished my book on history (*A Theory of History*) more than a decade ago, it became immediately clear to me that, though the book had been completed, the project had not. Our world is open-ended, and so are our projects.

The philosophical style of this volume differs from that of *A Theory of History*. I am in great sympathy with Richard Rorty's suggestion that one need not address all possible issues in the same style. There are different genres in philosophy to the same extent as in other branches of literature, and some allow for a better approach to certain problems than others. The viewpoint too makes a difference. For example, one can address various issues from a single unified viewpoint, one distinct issue from different viewpoints, or, lastly, divergent but interconnected issues from slightly different, yet interconnected, viewpoints. The first two ways of organization allow for a systematic approach while the third does not.

In a systematic or quasi-systematic approach, a work of philosophy has to be written in the style of a detective story. The authors must know who the murderer is in advance; they must put all their cards on the table at the end of their story so that the reader will be satisfied that the riddle has been solved – all the questions have been answered, all counter-arguments defeated. It is thus that the wonderful makebelieve of consistency has to be created. There is nothing wrong with strictly demonstrative or argumentative philosophies, nor can grand narratives be faulted in general. I do not even subscribe to the widespread opinion that philosophical genres with absolutist or foundationalist claims (for example, metaphysics) are altogether antiquated. My position is more modest. If one decides to address different but interconnected segments of life from slightly different (though interconnected) viewpoints, one cannot write philosophy in the style of a detective story, for the obvious reason: one cannot know the identity of the murderer in advance. This time it is impossible to put all the cards on the table at the end of the philosophical journey, if only because the whole pack has not yet been dealt.

I am familiar with three philosophical genres that are suitable for such an open-ended presentation: dialogue, essay and deconstruction. One of them, deconstruction, as an extremely rigid genre, is suitable only for thinkers who have developed a strong personal affinity for the rules of this particular game. Both dialogue and essay, however, allow the practice of a great variety of philosophical games, such as demon-stration, description, narration, analysis, dialectics, mild rhetoric, illustration. They can employ allegory, metaphor, historical example, scientific proof or something else. Equally, both allow for the resump-tion of a great variety of philosophical attitudes such as moralistic, critical, sceptical, ironical, persuasive, solemn, humorous, and slightly prophetic. What they still exclude are the two extreme attitudes of self-complacent dogmatism and self-devouring frivolousness.

The first essay ('Hermeneutics of Social Sciences') in this volume was written three years ago and has been slightly revised since. Actually, it was during my work on this topic, without having given a thought to this eventuality in advance, that it first occurred to me that modernity might not survive. When I discovered (for myself) the death wish right in the spiritual centre of modern imagination, I could not avoid taking it seriously. All the other essays grew out of the first, and they were all committed to paper in the last year and a half. They address various, though interconnected, issues from slightly different, yet interconnected, viewpoints. But the perspective of the essays, their underlying vision, is identical.

II

Sigmund Freud, who first coined the term, did not attribute the 'death wish' to old age. Yet the suicidal tendencies in nations and cultures are, as a rule, regarded as manifestations of spiritual exhaustion, the loss of vital forces, and are attributed to senility. Philosophers of culture of the last hundred years have promoted the image of a Europe or a 'West' that has arrived at the end of its historical mission. The increase in relativism, 'nihilism', libertarianism, tolerance, scepticism and much else was, and sometimes still is, seen as an unmistakable sign of a mortal disease.

The senility argument grew out of a biological metaphor. In order to enable us to speak of a cultural unit's youth or old age, at least its *identity* needs to be established. It makes sense to assert that the cultural, social and moral potentials of Rome were finally exhausted, regardless of whether one agrees or disagrees with the proposition. But to assert that the European culture has been exhausted with the emergence of modernity makes no sense at all. For a start, what is this entity called 'Europe' which was once young, then grew old, only to decline, precisely in modernity, into an irreversible senility? Is 'Europe' identical with the Greeks or the Romans, or rather with the Visigoths and the Vandals? Was the exhaustion, the old age, of Rome at the same time the vigorous youth of Europe? Cultural identity is always constructed and interpretively established in myths and in historical narratives. Modern Europe invented the grand narrative and has established its identity in an all too sovereign fashion. The 'cultural decay' narrative is the optimistic grand narrative in reverse. Of course, not even the most fantastic interpretive reconstruction is entirely lacking in empirical foundations. Certain factors must have been present in pre-modern Europe that made the emergence of modernity possible; or modernity would not have come about. Many splendid narratives have sprung from this commonplace and infinitely more will follow suit. Heidegger's story about metaphysics as the carrier of our cultural identity is only one of the current versions, if the most influential one. But there is also another commonplace to consider: a possibility does not entail its result. Neither the development of the forces of production, nor the victory of the Platonic metaphysics, nor Christianity nor anything else has 'resulted' in modernity. Modernity is not the 'old age' of the entity of a single body or spirit that has arrived at the last stage of its long journey, regardless of whether 'old age' stands for the consummation of accumulated wisdom or for irreversible senility.

The gist of the matter is that the 'death wish' at the heart of modernity does not result from Christianity (as Nietzsche would have it) or from Plato's state. One could make the assumption that a certain kind of 'death wish' resides in the heart of many a culture (not being a Freudian, I would not assert that in all cultures), but different cultures cope with it more or less successfully, in their own different ways. As modern men and women, we are primarily interested in our own way of coping with it as well as with the question of whether or not we can cope successfully.

Paradoxically, both hostile and complimentary narratives locate the sources of the modern 'death wish' mainly in liberalism, its side-effects and consequences (relativism, tolerance, loss of martial virtues, individualism, and the like). In the major narratives of decadence, tracing modern liberalism back to either Greece, Rome or Christianity serves the purpose of associating liberalism with senility. Once we have dismissed the grand narrative, nothing remains to support the association between modernity on the one hand and 'senility' on the other.

The old story can be replaced by an image of 'modernity' just recently born. And this is the common, unifying vision behind all the essays of this volume. They have sprung from the experience of 'amazement' (the Platonic *thaumadzein*) in looking at modernity as a brand-new experiment, one that was launched some two hundred years ago (which is practically yesterday by the yardstick of any history) and that is still in its period of trial and (grave) error. We can do justice to our chosen and continually reinterpreted cultural heritage and accept both the contingency and novelty of modernity in one breath. Once this has been done, all problems of our history will appear in a different and new light, including the puzzle of the 'death wish'. The issue under scrutiny will no longer be the demise of a senile culture, but rather the capacity (or incapacity) for survival of a brand-new social and political arrangement.

There is no knowledge concerning the capacity for survival of a historical newborn, precisely because it is an unprecedented arrangement. To echo Hegel, modernity is still an abstraction in the early phase of the process of 'concretization'. This is the question I address in detail in the essay 'The Concept of the Political' (Chapter 6). Modernity confronts us with puzzles rather than with solutions, with opaqueness rather than with transparency. Some would blame 'fetishism', others the increase in 'complexity', for these epistemic difficulties, all of which make complete sense. Still, the puzzles are not eliminated. I will mention only one of these remaining puzzles. The word 'difference' has never been uttered so frequently and with such an evaluative emphasis as in our age. Modernity does not merely tolerate, it positively cultivates difference. We make efforts to overcome the (historically) natural attitude of ethnocentrism, that of uncritical self-identification and the abuse of the alien. At the same time, differences disappear from our life with increasing speed. The more the modern lifestyle expands, the more uniform all human groups become. This phenomenon was well known to cultural critics of the last hundred years. Mass society, democracy and industrialization were blamed in turn for the loss of cultural singularity, distinction and difference. We can, alternatively, attribute the increase in uniformity to the 'abstractness' of modernity, to the circumstance that the process of self-differentiation is at its very beginning, whereas the withering differences are but remnants of the pre-modern, still hierarchical, form of life. But we simply do not know whether new cultural differences will ever actually develop in modernity. For uniformity could increase to the point where all cultural varieties have been reduced to the difference between the Singapore Hilton and the Vienna Hilton, or that of the taste of the tuna sandwich one can consume in both.

III

It is self-evident that there is no answer of absolute certitude to the question whether modernity can survive. Within a single systematic (or quasi-systematic) framework even the question cannot be properly illuminated. Hegel's metaphor of the owl of Minerva, which starts its flight only after darkness has fallen, and his follow-up metaphor of philosophy which paints grey in grey, together describe the status of the systematic approach to modernity in a nutshell. As long as modernity was still *in statu nascendi* on the European subcontinent, the 'riddle of history', to use Marx's term, appeared to have been solved or at least to be close to solution. The key to the riddle was thus supposed to have been handed over to philosophy and to the social sciences by history itself. Once modernity had settled in and expanded far beyond the European subcontinent and North America, the actual *present* became the main object of philosophical scrutiny. This present is not to be grasped as the outcome of the past or as a brief 'transitory period' towards an everlasting future. The key to the riddle of history has been lost on the way. In *A Theory of History* I indicated the emergence of this new historical consciousness, born out of confusion and slowly taking different shapes. These days, following the current vocabulary, I call this new historical consciousness 'post-modern'. Since I have repeatedly clarified my own understanding of post-modern consciousness, I do not see any reason why I should refrain from using the term just because others interpret 'post-modernity' in an entirely different fashion.

The question 'Can modernity survive?' is a post-modern question, but it is not asked *about* post-modernity, since such an 'epoch', at least in my mind, does not exist. Nor are there any signs to indicate its coming into being. The question is posed to modernity from the point of view of post-modern historical consciousness.

Post-modern consciousness turns towards itself. It is from our ways of life that the chances for the survival of modernity can be deciphered. And, in turn, our ways of life can best be approached through the forms of contemporary historical consciousness. I could have used the term 'contemporary discourse' instead. Post-modern consciousness is intrinsically dialogical, for it is impossible to conduct monologues from an authentically post-modern point of view. Monological philosophical thinking is grounded in the firm conviction that there is something completely objective 'out there' (for example, socio-historical laws) and that the mind can grasp it if only proper theories are devised and proper methods applied. But this conviction has been thoroughly shaken. We live under the spell of hermeneutics: hermeneutics and the awareness of intersubjectivity overdetermine one another. Due to this entanglement, subject(s) and object(s) can merge. Let me make the problem perfectly clear. Methodological scepticism can be intensified by increasing the distance between those who know and that which is known, also by multiplying the mediations between them so that apodictic statements can no longer be uttered. The discourse becomes more and more self-reflective and more and more method-conscious. Questions like 'How do we know that we know something?', 'How do we know that what we know is the very something that we know?', 'How do we know that what we know is better known by us than by others who know it otherwise?' are heaped upon each other. Methodological–epistemological over-reflexivity normally results in a kind of relativism (if we disregard academic hair-splitting). One can also arbitrarily stop the escalation of over-reflexivity and limit the scope of legitimate questioning. Such arbitrary barricades can be termed 'rationality' or 'reason' with full authority. They can also be erected with a royal gesture (as in Wittgenstein's case). Yet one can also choose not to erect barricades and just go ahead with the escalation of over-reflexivity towards its self-exhaustion. If too many 'as ifs' are heaped upon each other, if the number of 'reversals' and 'reversals of reversals' are knotted together in a way that no one can succeed in undoing them, the Gordian knot needs to be cut once again. This time, cutting the Gordian knot means leaving behind over-reflexivity, speaking again with authority without trying to legitimize the veracity of each and every statement. Over-reflexivity becomes so unbearable that it results in its apparent opposite, a kind of apodictic neo-naivety. I term this solution 'second naivety', using the expression of the young Lukacs.

Philosophers traditionally speak with authority because their way of warranting the veracity of their propositions is to relate them consistently to an absolute foundation. Critical philosophy has discredited this 'naive' approach, and the philosophies of 'second naivety' are simply not in a position to return to the pre-critical fold. Here over-reflexivity ceases to be methodological, which is why thinkers can now commence their philosophical story at any point and without the obligation of first presenting their credentials. But, in a manner of speaking, the same over-reflexivity is now projected onto the world. The twists and turns, the reversals and the reversals of reversals, become embedded in the story itself. It is sometimes difficult to fathom the 'position' of the author or whether the author has any position at all. The philosopher of 'second naivety' speaks with authority. This authority rests in the philosopher as a *subject*. (What a subject now is, is discussed in the essay 'Death of the Subject?' – Chapter 3). One could agree with the Lukács of *The Theory of the Novel* that the subjects', that is the 'the problematic individual's', point of view is at its best in story-telling. Post-modern philosophy indeed shows a predilection for story-telling. The stories differ from the grand narratives not in being shorter or more modest or less fantastic but in resigning the claim to have solved the celebrated riddle of history once and for all. Without doubt, this is a manifestation of the standpoint of the subject. And yet philosophical stories are not fictions, or at least not in the same sense as novels are. The philosopher still dwells in the medium of thinking, and it is always *something* that one thinks. Kant insisted that thinking is tantamount to coming to know things through concepts. If 'coming to know' includes understanding, making sense, interpretation, contemplating and much else, we can still subscribe to this tentative quasi-definition. The lavish use of metaphors, similes and the like does not degrade, nor does it elevate the philosophical approach of 'second naivety'. It remains an exercise in conceptual thinking, even though each story is stamped with the cachet of its author more than ever before, and despite the fact that every author will tell his or her own stories. But all stories are told about our world, or from the aspect of our world, and there will perforce be decisive common elements in all of them. These common elements are the 'objects' of the story: they embody the shared visions of our age about itself. What I termed the identity of subject(s) and object(s) is the merger of one person's idiosyncratic vision with one of the shared visions of our self-understanding. The (post-)modern story-teller can resume an apodictic approach and can project all methodological complications back onto the world, precisely because his or her authority is personal ('I see it this way, this is my story'), and also interpersonal as far as the story-teller manifests a shared vision to an extent that makes the personal story plausible for others. (The relation of plausibility and truth is discussed in the first essay of the volume.) This is how (post-)modern narratives overcome relativism.

IV

I raised the question of whether modernity can survive with the resolve to avoid supplying a strongly rhetorical answer. Strong rhetoric is the easiest exercise. One wishes something (for example, one strongly desires the survival of modernity), and one 'proves' one's case. Demonstration, argumentation, all the traditional empirical and rational procedures can as easily employ strong rhetoric as do narratives, grand or small.

One can avoid strong rhetoric if one decides not to beat about the bush: I strongly wish that modernity should survive. I have elaborated my distinction between pre-modern and modern in the main in the essays 'Everyday Life' (Chapter 2) and 'Rights, Modernity, Democracy' (Chapter 8), and the reader has not been left in the dark about my allegiances. This commitment is not based on the idea of a progressive development of 'universal history', or on the expectation of mere gains without losses. I prefer the modern arrangement to the pre-modern one because it embodies relations of symmetric reciprocity and because it offers the conditions of freedom simply by throwing men and women back on their contingency. I am aware that these two constituents of modernity, along with some others, are the major blemishes of modernity in the eyes of those who desire its demise. Subjectively, I doubt the authenticity of such an approach in most cases for the simple reason that those great advocates of the pre-modern arrangement invariabley project themselves back into the position of free Athenian male citizens or of medieval feudal lords or bishops, and never into the life and situation of Athenian women, slaves, medieval servants or serfs. Still, commitment to modernity by no means includes a commitment to everything that is modern and the rejection of everything that is not. One can bemoan the demise of many things that are beautiful, noble and elegant, and still be satisfied that the social arrangements that had given birth to them are gone. The servant loyal to this master till death may evoke our admiration and empathy but not the wish to resurrect the actual world based on the predominance of the master–servant relationship.

The question concerning the chances for survival of modernity cannot be severed from other questions concerning the quality of life in modernity. Qualities of life are not accidental predicates casually pinned to the subject of survival. Freedom is the central modern value, and the interpretation and determination of freedom is what modern politics is all about. I discuss this issue in the essay 'The Concept of the Political Revisited' (Chapter 6). The value of freedom is fundamental at all levels and in all niches of modern life, not just in political contestation. When modern men and women discuss survival, they have in mind the survival of certain qualities of life, which, directly or indirectly, all embrace freedom. Mere survival can be the main value for single individuals, even for single human groups, for a while, but it cannot be the leading value of modernity. To formulate the same thought in reverse: if survival became the highest and most universal value, the social arrangement called 'modernity' would already have been left behind.

No single model of a supreme way of life exists in modernity nor is modernity a 'totality'. Modern men and women experience their world as brittle and they try to inject as much unity into it as they can or as they deem fit for themselves. Accordingly, the essays in this volume do not pretend to constitute a 'totality' in their entirety. Yet they all approach one or another quality of the modern life; this is how they belong together. Their final unity is projected by my approach. Since I wish modernity to survive, because I wish that the quality of freedom should unfold its potential in full within the social arrangement of symmetric reciprocity, I cannot pretend to have avoided weak rhetoric.

The genre of the philosophical essay offers a fair amount of scope for stylistic variations, particularly if one takes up the position of 'second naivety', which is not a doctrinaire position. Those adopting it are not compelled to stay within jealously guarded stylistic boundaries. Every essay can have its own style. Some of the essays in this volume, particularly those concerning politics and ethics, are argumentative at least in part. Others, especially those that address issues of everyday life or personal life, are closer to a straightforward narrative. For example, the essay on emotional wealth or impoverishment (Chapter 4) was written in a free-floating narrative style and almost concluded on a note of happy ending. Some of the essays require bibliographic references, others do not. But all of them, the more argumentative as well as the more narrative ones, those that refer approvingly or disapprovingly to the writings of contemporary authors and those that do not, stand alike in the midst of contemporary debates and participate in them.

Affinities between topic and style manifest also the author's approach and vision. Matters of politics or ethics are not 'objectively' better suited to an argumentative approach than other subject matters. Two essays of this volume, 'The Concept of the Political Revisited' (Chapter 6) and 'What Is Practical Reason, and What Is It Not' (Chapter 5), are more confrontationalist than the others because they deal with issues of practical reason, and because in my mind issues of theoretical, interpretive relevance and issues of directly practical relevance need to be strongly differentiated. No harm is done, and perhaps a degree of freedom of play and imagination is achieved if interpretations of the human condition and of the actual present take the form of fairly idiosyncratic narratives, and if the intersubjective character or value of those narratives become manifest in the course of reception. But in ethics and politics, in these two directly practical relations between actors, at least a minimum of intersubjective agreement needs to precede personal decisions, and the play of imagination needs to be enhanced, as much as limited, by those agreements (values, norms). A world without a minimum of political and ethical consensus cannot survive, at least not as a meaningful arrangement. The essay form does not allow for the elaboration of this theme. But the theme shapes the character of the essay.

This volume is a contribution to an open-ended discussion: it does not begin at the beginning nor does it end where it is concluded. Had I chosen a subtitle for the book, it would have read as follows: 'A year and a half of conversations.'

1
Hermeneutics of Social Science

I

A new type of historical consciousness, both reflected and universal, emerged during the Enlightenment and has become dominant since the French Revolution. Western men and women embarked on an understanding of their age in terms of its being a product of world-historical progression, where each stage contained its own possibilities and limitations as well as being superseded in turn by another stage. Hegel constructed a grand philosophical edifice on this new ground of self-understanding. No one has ever transcended and no one will ever transcend, he contended, in action, thought, project, fantasy or utopia, *his own* Time; we shall not be able to do so either. Yet, Hegel added, the past that we are able to recollect from the peak of our present is the *Whole*, that is, the whole History and the *whole Truth*.[1] The Hegelian time capsule carries a dual paradox that only the Hegelian system was momentarily able to sublate. Reflected universalism had given birth to Faustian Man, who overthrows all taboos and transcends all limits, who is eager to know everything, to act out all his projects and desires. However, the same reflected universality publicly declared that we are captives of the prisonhouse of contemporaneity. Reflected universalism had transformed Truth into 'historical Truth', robbing the world of the eternal, the timeless, without ever being able to quench the thirst for certitude in both the outer and inner worlds. Modern historical consciousness inherently encompasses this dual paradox, just as well as all the attempts to live with it and bear with it proudly.

The quest for understanding and self-understanding includes the quest for knowing present history, the historical present, our own society as ourselves. One is confronted with the task of obtaining *true knowledge* about a *world* whilst being aware that this knowledge is situated in that world. How can one know that one's knowledge is true? How can one know that one knows? In order to overcome the paradox, an Archimedean point outside contemporaneity must be found. However, this is exactly what cannot be done: the prisonhouse of the present allows for only illusory escape.

Even so, one escape route has indeed remained open. Let us suppose that our history and our historical consciousness, and these things alone, create certain language games or methods that provide contemporary men and women with Archimedean points outside the boundaries of contemporaneity. Under these conditions, the paradox will prove unreal, a mere semblance. Language games like this are termed 'social sciences'. Both nomothetic and hermeneutic social sciences offer an Archimedean point, albeit ones different in kind. Let us first take nomothetic (or explanatory) social sciences. Suppose we can establish certain general historical-social laws or regularities that, once discovered, can be applied to *all* histories and all societies, ours included. Thus our own history, our own institutions, our society can be explained, and so understood, fully and truly. We overcome the limits of our historical consciousness by using the potentials of that same historical consciousness. Hermeneutic sciences will yield a similar result. Suppose we can converse with actors of bygone ages or with members of alien cultures; let us further suppose that we are able to read the minds of these people (or their texts) and come to know what they really meant (or mean). Finally, let us assume that owing to all this we are able to look back at ourselves with these very alien eyes, from the cultural context of this 'other'. If only we can make these 'others' raise *their* questions, and assess and judge our history and institutions from their perspective, in other words their historical consciousness, we will have established an Archimedean point *outside* our own culture. Here, again, we overcome the limits of our own historical consciousness by mobilizing its own potentials. Thus nomothetic and hermeneutic social sciences alike are products of our historical consciousness. Both have expressed the awareness of our historicity; both have originated as formidable attempts to provide true self-knowledge for an epoch that understands itself as historical. The increasing awareness of the complexity and fallibility of the undertaking termed 'social science' did not shake the belief in the ultimate success of this undertaking itself. It is only now, in the period termed 'post-modern', that the scene has been reset. That is why the compound term 'social sciences' itself has been put under hermeneutic scrutiny.

In the process of a progressive division of the cultural spheres in modernity, the social sciences have established themselves in the dominant sphere, that of science. Weber, whose vision of the division of cultural spheres is a lucid rendering of the modern condition, discusses science as a vocation,[2] though he had in mind only social sciences. With certain provisos, one can still subscribe to the Weberian diagnosis as well as to his interdictions. Science, Weber contended, is one cultural sphere alongside the political, legal, aesthetic, economic, religious and erotic spheres. The relative independence of each sphere results from, and is the precondition of, the reproduction of modernity. Each sphere contains norms and rules intrinsic to itself and different from the norms and rules of the other spheres. If, for example, the intrinsic norms and rules of the political sphere or the economic sphere, or for that matter of the aesthetic sphere, were to be applied to and observed in the sphere of science, the proper norms of the latter would be curtailed, and science would be distorted. Yet it should be noted that spheric distinction depends also on our perception. Though social sciences have never really *behaved* like natural sciences, it is only in the last fifty years or so that we have become aware of this fact. The natural sciences, despite changes of paradigm, proved to be essentially cumulative, whereas the social sciences, despite the tendency to build up certain kinds of knowledge, proved to be essentially non-cumulative, although they claimed to be all-embracingly cumulative.

Knowledge can be cumulative in so far as the intrinsic langauge game is pre-eminently one of problem-solving. X has solved a problem, I can rely upon this solution, I can go on and solve the next problem, and so on. In the social sciences, this would mean, for example, that Marx solves a problem, Tonnies relies on this solution and goes one step further, Weber, relying on both of these efforts, goes a great deal further. Parsons inherits all these solutions and adds his own to the list, whilst, in the present, Luhmann builds upon the solutions of all the preceding sociologists in his research, and so on. This sounds like, and indeed is, a parody. The reason for the parodic character of this assumption is simply that social sciences are not predominantly concerned with problem solving in the first place. They create meaning and they contribute to our self-knowledge. They address problems, they elucidate them, they place them into one context or another, and in so far as they do solve problems, which they certainly do, they solve them within this broad and overarching context. In social sciences there is no such thing as *the* final solution to a problem, not even when working within the framework of one and the same paradigm. In this respect the social sciences are akin to philosophy, and not to the natural sciences. From Dilthey onwards, hermeneutics has been well aware of this.

Social sciences can establish an independent sphere of their own (after being divorced from natural sciences), and can renounce the claim to cumulative knowledge and exactitude. Yet there is one claim they certainly cannot renounce: the claim that they can provide true knowledge about society, in particular about our own modern society. If they withdrew this claim they would undoubtedly cease to exist. In social sciences, meaning is related to, or rather 'wrung out of', true knowledge. History, Ranke insists, should narrate events as they *really* happened, and sociology, in terms of Max Weber's imperative, should construct ideal types that enable us to understand how institutions *really* work. On this point, whether or not historians, sociologists, or social scientists of any other hue can completely fulfil this norm is irrelevant. Moreover, norms, in contrast to rules, can be observed in different ways. The gist of the matter is that the norm of verisimilitude must be observed or else social science no longer exists. Yet if there is no problem-solving in social sciences (or if problem-solving plays a subordinate role), if there is no cumulative knowledge in social sciences other than in the area of publications, how can the claim to verisimilitude be redeemed?

First, this can be done by avoiding misunderstandings. Nietzsche once said that science had been invented in order to fend off Truth. In Heidegger's rendition, the original Greek insight into the character of Truth as *aletheia* (unconcealment) had, in modern philosophy and modern sciences, been replaced by the correspondence theory of Truth. True knowledge alias 'mirroring' alias correctness occupied the place of Truth. Certain branches of philosophy, in particular those with positivist leanings, are indeed guilty of this crude blunder, and social scientists too have followed suit. However, the quest for true knowledge itself can neither fend off Truth nor 'conceal' it – Truth and true knowledge are simply different in kind. True knowledge *can* become Truth (other conditions, yet to be elaborated on, having been met), but it cannot become Truth simply by presenting itself as true knowledge. The greatest social scientists have always been the least likely to confuse true knowledge with Truth. Weber, who denounced this fallacy as a dangerous delusion, is an obvious example. Weber clearly warned his students *not* to seek insight into the meaning of life in their pursuit of the social sciences: the search for true knowledge must be chosen as a vocation and not as a path leading to Truth. To offer insight into Truth through the pursuit of true knowledge is to make a false promise, one that the social sciences have no authority to keep.

If this most serious of misunderstandings is avoided, there are still serious questions to be faced. How can one live up to the norm of verisimilitude? How can one ascertain whether one has done so? The matter can be summed up in the following question: what are the criteria of true knowledge, the criteria of verisimilitude, in the social sciences? If we succeed in finding these criteria, we can be satisfied that we have sufficiently – though not completely – understood social sciences.

II

Although modern sciences are supposed to stand under the Cartesian spell, whoever casts a dispassionate glance at the history of social sciences will see that the latter have never fully subscribed to the rationalistic criteria of Truth as developed during the seventeenth century by Descartes, Spinoza or even Hobbes. The advice given by the great rationalists, that we should throw away all books because reading only fills our minds with falsities and prejudices, could not be heeded in social science. Nor could the social sciences live up to the other methodological imperative, that of deducing all their statements from a few axioms. To 'know something' in the sphere of social sciences at least *included* the knowledge of certain texts. Even the most dedicated attempts at mathematizing certain branches of social science stopped short of being fully rationalistic–deductive. And, as noted by Anthony Giddens, mere empiricist methods did not fare much better.[3] To mention only one obstacle, the so-called factual material in social science is never completely based on observation. Nowadays, 'knowing something in the sphere of social sciences' is associated more with 'having a great deal of information', being 'widely read', being 'knowledgeable' and so forth. One need not be pleased with this development to agree that being 'knowledgeable' constitutes at least one aspect of 'having true knowledge' in the social sciences, a factor that Descartes would certainly have regarded as a sign of complete ignorance. The element of the great rationalist tradition that has remained effective is the 'Cartesian moment' manifest in every scientific inquiry. By 'Cartesian moment' I mean what Kant termed *Selbstdenken*, something that is tantamount to the attitude of not accepting any text, statement or presentation as representing *un-contestable* authority. For knowledge can be true only if it is also condoned by the researcher's own reason.

There is yet another Cartesian legacy that cannot be completely abandoned in the social sciences. Although social scientists cannot possibly subscribe to the Cartesian tenet that the clarity and distinctness of a notion that is present in one's mind must be taken as proof of its veracity, they must still keep their notions as clear and distinct as their medium permits. In social science one can only rarely use 'real definitions' in a reasonable manner, since the more central and the more crucial a social concept is, the less this concept can be defined. Should one choose to define notions like 'society', 'work', 'culture', and the like, one will immediately come to realize that these definitions will be completely empty, and therefore either insignificant in the quest for true knowledge or incapable of being consistently applied in this quest. Of course, a nominal definition can always be provided, and such definitions fulfil a proper orientative function, but they have no cognitive value and do not contribute to our knowledge, whether this knowledge is true or false. This is why Weber recommended *Bestimmung* (determination) instead of definition in sociology. *Bestimmung* makes concepts as clear as possible only in so far as the notion thus determined provides the identity of the notion prevailing in all uses and interpretations, but it also indicates something more or less than or different from what we ourselves have chosen to indicate. The aspect of non-identity is further highlighted by the circumstance that even the consistent use of the notion can and will be viewed as not entirely consistent by those looking at this matter from a different perspective. In short, the social sciences do not only open themselves up to falsification, which all sciences do; they also open themselves up to interpretation–reinterpretation.

What has apparently begun here in the usual apologetic manner ('social sciences cannot be completely deductive or totally inductive', 'they cannot offer a clear and distinct definition of their own basic notions') has finished on a positive note: with the social sciences we are dealing with branches of knowledge that are open to interpretation and reinterpretation. Significant works of social science are treasure-troves that we always revisit in our quest for meaning and true knowledge.

Let me reiterate that the quest for true knowledge in the social sciences is coterminous with reconstructing, depicting, narrating, modelling, understanding, interpreting 'how it really happened', 'how it really works', 'how it was really meant', 'how it was really understood', and so on. Irrespective of whether events, institutions or other things are primarily interpreted or explained, both the interpretation and explanation must be plausible. It has frequently been noted that, in social sciences, probability or plausibility amounts to verisimilitude. The act of proving, Collingwood says,[4] is the translation of the Latin *probare*, which can also be rendered as 'making plausible'. And here we reach a significant parting of the ways: while I accept that verisimilitude can be rendered in terms of plausibility, I do not accept that plausibility in a general sense is a sufficient criterion of true knowledge in social sciences.

It is equally common knowledge that plausibility is also a central category of rhetoric. I would add to this that plausibility and probability make a theory true in everyday thinking as well. If theories in social sciences are true in so far as they are plausible, then the criteria of verisimilitude would prove to be identical in rhetoric, social sciences and everyday life. Since this is a less than promising starting point, we could extend our search for a criterion for social science that is stronger than that of plausibility. Yet this criterion could only be that of certitude, a criterion we have rejected at this preliminary stage. In this apparent impasse, the answer seems to be that we need not go beyond plausibility, but we should look for a specific type of criterion of plausibility. Briefly, what makes a theory plausible in rhetoric and everyday life is a set of procedures that are not identical with those making a theory plausible in the social sciences.

Verisimilitude is the result of social enquiry, and this enquiry must be guided by certain norms. One of these norms can be formulated as follows: social science should not use the addressee as the means to achieve certain goals of the social scientists. One uses the addressee as a means if one formulates a theory such that the addressee acts in a manner the social theorist wants, desires, wishes or wills them to act in mobilizing certain emotive responses or playing upon certain interests of the addressee. This interdiction is both practical (moral) and theoretical. It is practical (moral) because, if the addressee is used in the manner outlined, he or she becomes the object of manipulation (which is exactly what strong rhetoric is all about). The interdiction is equally valid on the theoretical plane, because in respect of strong rhetoric the theory will be completely plausible for the addressee but for one one else. Furthermore, even for the addressee it will remain plausible only as long as the emotions and interests the theorist plays upon remain charged. This is why heavily rhetorical theories can be extremely influential in their original context but quickly decline to the level of being mere historical documents, and do not show evidence of the paradigmatic appeal that the theories we have called the 'treasure-troves' of the social sciences show.

However, the interdiction on strong rhetoric in social sciences does not entail the interdiction on evaluation. There is no need for either non-rhetorical or mildly rhetorical social theories to be 'value-free'. I have repeatedly expressed my agreement with Weber that the social sciences should observe the norms of their own sphere and that the norms of other cultural spheres should not encroach upon the norms of social science. By this I did not mean to assert that values inherent in the other spheres cannot inform enquiry in the realm of social sciences or that they cannot provide a critical standpoint from which an enquiry can be conducted. Many different, albeit equally plausible and equally scientific, theories can coexist, one theory being informed by one value of one sphere, another theory being anchored in a different value of yet another sphere. Yet living up to the internal norms of social sciences is an Ought for each theory alike, for the constitution of a theory is one thing and the manipulation of the addressee is another. When, for example, Weber insisted that social scientists should always make a careful inventory of so-called 'unpleasant facts' (those that question or undermine their own theories), he made a good case against strong rhetoric, but not against evaluation, as he believed he had. This is simply because facts are not inherently pleasant or unpleasant, but *become* pleasant or unpleasant from the standpoint of the guiding value of a particular theory. The same fact that is extremely embarrassing for one social scientist can be providential for another social scientist.

Therefore, even if plausibility and verisimilitude are not equated, and one looks for the criteria of plausibility specific to social sciences, one must conclude that there exists more than one plausible, and in that sense scientific, social theory concerning the same issue, institution, event, and so on. This circumstance in itself would be a sufficient reason for not equating verisimilitude (a particular kind of plausibility) with 'correspondence'. Human events and institutions are not simply 'there' to be mirrored as a 'true picture on the retina', as the metaphor suggests. Members of a particular institution perceive this institution in a thousand different ways, and the same applies to the participants of a particular event. And what is not completely identical in the perception of the participant cannot be completely identical from the viewpoint of the observer, and this is especially so considering there are no 'pure' observers either. Whoever is an observer, whoever takes the position of mere theoretical reason, is, at the same time, a participant member of certain institutions and spheres *other* than the institution or the sphere of social science – at the very least this person participates in the sphere of everyday life.

From all this it follows (a) that verisimilitude cannot be tantamount to correspondence, because there is no single thing 'there' that true knowledge should correspond to, and (b) that a certain aspect of correspondence must be present in that the very existence and 'thusness' of the interpreted facts must be corroborated by every type of interpretation and theory concerned with it. And so, to put it somewhat crudely, and also briefly, verisimilitude in social sciences can be understood as the identity of identity and non-identity. A work that is a product of the social sciences could thus be said to contain a core and a ring, not as two separate parts of a theory but as its two aspects. To avoid misunderstanding, I wish to state that the 'core aspect' is not identical with the sum total of interpreted facts, and the 'ring' aspect is not identical with the general theoretical framework used by social scientists. For example, in writing about the role of the United States in World War II, one can discuss the intentions of President Roosevelt without believing that these interpreted facts belong to the 'core knowledge' of this particular event. Core knowledge is knowledge of the type that one has good reason to believe that any person would arrive at, if this person studied all the available sources, thoroughly observed the relevant phenomena, entered into discussion with the members of the scientific community familiar with the matter under scrutiny, and undertook these things from any perspective whatsoever. Ring knowledge is knowledge (insight, theory, interpretation, understanding) of the kind one arrives at from a particular standpoint, perspective or cultural interest not shared with others, against the backdrop of certain life experiences, individual or collective. This is why one cannot even surmise that anyone else would have arrived at the same insight, theory, interpretation, understanding, in a word: knowledge. Even less can one surmise that *everyone* would have arrived at such a point. 'Ring knowledge' has a special capacity to render meaning because it brings the elements of originality, innovation, novelty, surprise, in other words, elements of the unexpected, of imagination, into the core. If, in relation to the core, the ring is too thin, the knowledge provided by a particular work of social science will be unexciting, albeit true; unimportant, albeit informative. If, in relation to the core, the ring is too wide, too thick, the work in question will be more a work of fiction or ideology than one of social science proper. I should stress here that core knowledge too is open to falsification.

Keeping the 'core' and the 'ring', the 'identity elements' and the 'non-identity elements within identity', in the right balance is one of the most formidable tasks of modern social science, if not *the* most formidable task. Modern social sciences are under a twofold pressure. First, they are under pressure in so far as an immense accumulation of information has recently occurred in these sciences, an accumulation of a kind that has very little or nothing to do with a cumulative progress in problem-solving so untypical in social science proper. The social scientist is under pressure to include every bit of information concerning his or her topic; irrespective of whether the reference is approving or disapproving, whether the information is later simply brushed aside or ignored, such references must be made. Considered approval or disapproval is of course a matter of judgement, and as such is related to the researcher's perspective ('the ring'). Yet it is practically impossible to think over, to assess or to evaluate every bit of information from one or another perspective. What remains is an undigested lump of information, resulting in an inflation of the 'core'.

There is also another countervailing tendency or pressure. Because not everyone can be expected to be innovative and original, social scientists are at least expected to follow a trend, to indicate their allegiance to one of the latest fashions, to what is *le dernier cri*. Thus everyone sets about enlarging both the core and the ring. And this can be done, if at all, by substantially narrowing the scope of enquiry.

What is the proper balance between the 'identity elements' and the 'non-identity elements' within identity, between the 'core' and the 'ring'? There is no general answer to this question: such an assessment depends on the *phronesis* of the social scientists. As Aristotle once remarked, the proper measure, the 'middle measure', is located between the 'too little' and the 'too much'. The norms of the particular cultural sphere termed 'social science' behave as any other norms do: they must be applied, and applied differently, according to the task at hand. In actual fact, social scientists do mobilize their *phronesis*, and the best of them hit the mark. Proper proportion depends on many factors, one of them being, to use Croce's expression, 'the field of vision' encompassed by the work. Last but not least, there are many branches of social science and all of them *also* have their own intrinsic norms, whether strong or weak. Also, 'genre norms' can be dissolved, and new norms (or styles) established. One can even conceive of a *Gesamtwissenschaft* in social sciences after the analogy of *Gesamtkunst*. However, as long as a genre remains social science, to the extent that it does so, the constitution or the 'unconcealment' of Truth cannot be either intended or pretended by it.

I have now emphasized the distinction between the pursuit of true knowledge and the pursuit of Truth twice, for I hold this to be a matter of the greatest importance. It is precisely the false identification of true knowledge and Truth that has brought true knowledge into disrepute in recent philosophical discussions. To state my case fully, I should address the question of Truth, an endeavour outside the framework of this essay. I must, therefore, restrict myself to a few clarifying remarks. Everyday language users refer to a kind of knowledge, metaphor, symbol, experience and insight as 'truth', if the knowledge, metaphor, symbol, experience and so on impacts upon their whole existence. Truth is indeed 'the whole', not because it is about totality but because it concerns our existence as a whole. In this sense, Truth is always subjective. In everyday life this can signify 'truth-for-me'. If I have X-rays taken to determine whether I have cancer, the doctor will turn to the radiologist and ask, 'What is on the film?', in other words he will ask, 'What is the case?', but if I suspect the worst I will turn to the doctor and say, 'Tell me the truth'. Religion – in particular the Jewish, Christian, Buddhist, Moslem and Taoist religions – and philosophy (together with other branches of secular wisdom) search for a kind of knowledge, a myth, a symbol, and the like, which impacts upon the existence of all, which renders meaning to the lives of all of us, and in this sense can be called 'holistic'. 'Truth' is not merely theoretical. It is also practical (moral). Yet it is never pragmatic. Truth can be viewed as absolute, as perennial and also as historical, but it is always subjective in the sense that it impacts upon our whole existence. As we have seen, the quest for true knowledge has a different ambition. To live up to its ambition, to its own project, is the only requirement the fulfilment of which can be expected from social science – nothing else. But this still remains a great ambition, a crucial project.

III

As mentioned before, the more decisive, central, 'existential' a category is, the less it lends itself to definition. What 'understanding' means depends on the theory in the context of which the category is used. Because this notion will be *bestimmt* (determined, not defined) in the actual process of this discussion, I can say at this point only that my understanding of understanding will, at least in this context, fit the purpose of this essay. I will not use the concept in its broadest philosophical sense, i.e. one existential of *Dasein* or one constituent of the 'human condition', unless I explictly so state. But I will not identify understanding with interpretation either (both notions are English translations of the German *verstehen*), because to my mind every interpretation is also understanding, but not every understanding is interpretation. What we understand, we need not interpret. There is a fair amount of shared understanding among people of the same culture that remains unreflected, and thus uninterpreted, not only in everyday communication but also in the social sciences. (Although, of course, this background consensus too can be opened up for interpretation.) In addition, I will discuss both the quest for explanation and interpretation as subcases of the quest for understanding. To clarify this point I wish to say that understanding (in the context of social sciences) stands not only for 'making sense' but also for 'making sense of something that makes sense', or at least 'making sense of certain aspects that also "make sense" in the object-context of the particular enquiry'. This is why explanation in social science can be viewed as 'understanding' in a way that cannot occur in natural science. For example, it is assumed that the so-called 'law of value' (a merely explanatory device) manifests itself in a way that 'makes sense' for those selling and buying. But it cannot be surmised that the law of gravitation 'makes sense' for the apple. It becomes obvious from all this that, in addressing the problem of understanding, we still continue the discourse on true knowledge in social science.

When can we say that we understand something? Habermas asserts that a person understands something upon acquiring the competence to do the thing.[5] Rorty insists that, if we understand the language game, we have understood all there is to understand about why the moves in that particular language game are made.[6] These two suggestions are different in kind, yet they have two characteristics in common. Both writers discuss understanding as the understanding of rules, and rules alone, and both suggest that there is a point when we arrive at understanding, and that such a point can be correctly identified and described.

However, even if the presence of rules is taken for granted, the situation is already, in the sphere of the everyday, far more complex than is indicated above. To be sure, being competent to do something requires that I should understand rules to the degree that enables me to do what I am supposed (required) to do. And yet it is quite possible for someone to be completely competent and still not fully understand the rules themselves. An example of this is Thomas Mann's Felix Krull. If a friend gives me advice, I indeed understand the language game of 'giving advice'. However, it certainly does not follow from this that I have also understood *why* he gave me this particular piece of advice, and why he gave it to me on this and not another matter. It is also possible for a person to follow the rules but at the same time rebel against them in mind and heart. Furthermore, because social life is not only rule- but also norm-regulated, the same norms can be fulfilled in different ways and, within certain limits, fulfilled equally well (in the right way). To understand why this and not that has been done in a particular situation is an ongoing task, a matter full of guesswork, unlike in cases of mere rule-regulation.

Understanding is relational in the sense that it is relative to the actors or the actor's project. As phenomenologists, and Schutz in particular, have pointed out, the same level of understanding can be sufficient in one case and insufficient in another.[7] I have understood when I cease the quest for understanding because I need not (or alternatively cannot) go further. Yet whatever the level of understanding, there is always something that remains un-understood. As we have known since the time of Socrates, the higher the level of understanding, the more man's mind will be haunted by the lack thereof. Behind what has been understood there is always the mystery, the question mark, obscurity, the unvisited territory of attraction and repulsion. A remote acquaintance we may understand very well, but the mind of the closest friend eludes us, remains an eternal riddle. The closer a work of art to our heart, the less we will ever fully understand it.[8] As long as social institutions or historical events are 'taken for granted', we understand them to some degree. The moment we put them under scrutiny we start to understand what they really are all about, we begin our quest, and we will never stop. The more importance a particular institution, way or life or historical event carries for the historical consciousness of our age, the less it can be completely understood, irrespective of frequent 'final' and 'definitive' explanations furnished by social scientists. It was at the juncture of the traditional and the modern ways of life that Hebel's Master Anton, in *Mary Magdalene*, cried out in despair, '*Ich verstehe die Welt nicht mehr!*' (I no longer understand the world!)

Social sciences, these modern language games *par excellence*, have a contact point precisely with the modern ways of life, with the modern attitude of everyday actors. They promise the illumination of the incomprehensible and the opaque, they promise to provide modern society with self-knowledge, yet they enter exactly the same spiral path that everyday actors enter in their questioning of their own traditional ways of understanding.[9] The more social sciences proceed with their 'spiral of understanding', the more they shed light on the impenetrably opaque character of our social life. Certain social theories attempt to overcome these difficulties by construing the modern world as a complex of rule-governed institutions. Pure systems theories are of this provenance. The price they pay is that of severing the nexus between the life experiences and concerns of actors on the one hand and those of social theories on the other. They pay this price because they do not involve the actors (irrespective of whether they are passive readers or participant members of modern institutions) in their quest for true knowledge, but rather present them with a description of the rules and systemic constraints these actors are subject to. Thus the problem of increasing opacity, as it appears in the context of the quest, is being eliminated by making the entire world, the proper abode of the actors, 'taken for granted' for them, and as a result of this the latter will either cease their quest or face a totally incomprehensible social universe.

All this already indicates that 'understanding' in the social sciences implies 'making oneself understood'. This is not the case everywhere, and, even where it is, it is not the case to the same extent. A mystical experience (which is understanding of a kind) cannot properly be made understood. Further, I can try to understand my best friend without having the slightest intention of making my understanding understood by anyone else. To give a totally contrasting example, in pre-reflective everyday practice, understanding and 'making oneself understood' *completely* coalesce. In modern everyday life, once we have progressed beyond the pattern of self-evident pre-reflective understanding, we by and large behave in the same way that things take place in the social sciences: we take great pains to learn how to make something that has been understood by us understood by someone else.

Symmetric reciprocity requires mutual understanding. In discussing anthropology, MacIntyre points out that the symmetric reciprocity of communication (mutual understanding) can come about if, and only if, we can repeat in our own language what the members of another culture assert, and vice versa.[10] Without a mutual translatability of meanings, mutual understanding remains out of reach; however, short of mutual understanding we cannot understand each other because we cannot make ourselves understood. It is unnecessary to go as far as anthropology, the communication between two completely different cultures; translatability is the condition of proper understanding in sociology, political science and the other sciences as well. In other words, the language of the observer must be properly translatable into the language of the participant member of the institution under examination. Without the fulfilment of this (minimal) requirement, the observer will not succeed in making himself or herself understood at all. Moreover, social scientists must reach the point where both the process (the *modus operandi*) and the result of their enquiry are properly understood by the broader public. To make myself clearer, the social scientist is not obliged to formulate ideas and results in a way that is accessible to all. The social scientists is not even obliged to perform the work of translation. However, falling short of translatability means infringing an important norm of social science.

The limits to understanding, in relation to which social science is no exception, have been frequently pointed out. The quest for understanding continues against the backdrop of non-understanding, opacity and incomprehensibility. Yet there is a very special limit to this quest in the realm of the social sciences that has not yet been mentioned. The boundary of the authority of social science is the very boundary of the cultural sphere of social science: the self-understanding of society, of 'the objective spirit'. This authority extends to other cultural spheres (absolute spirit) only because all cultural spheres are co-constitutive of the life and consciousness of society. The sociology of art has no authority in the area of aesthetic values, just as the sociology of religion has no authority in the area of religious values. Moreover, sociological, anthropological and historical enquiries are normally conducted by people who do not share the life experience of those whose cultural institutions they seek to understand, especially not the childhood experiences of these people. A completely accurate translation cannot be achieved.

Every social scientist (as an individual repository of the sphere of social science) must deal with his or her own hermeneutic spiral. One returns to the same issue or problem again and again, understanding something a little more, understanding something in a different way, but always being painfully aware of falling short of a full understanding. The only thing that determines the point at which a social scientist should cease the quest for understanding is his or her good judgement, his or her *phronesis*. In finding the 'proper measure' between the 'too little' and the 'too much', there are no 'objective criteria' to follow. At the same time, it is down to the norm of social science to attempt to be sincere about the limits of our understanding and not to overstep the authority of this language game.

Nevertheless, even if all the above provisos about limitations are heeded, understanding in social science does, and always will, involve misunderstanding. The dialectic of understanding and misunderstanding in social science is not to be equated with the relation between understanding and non-understanding. To this matter I now turn.

IV

Every understanding involves misunderstanding; every interpretation involves misinterpretation. Understanding and interpretation are not coterminous, but they are intrinsically interrelated. I have circumscribed ('determined') my use of the term 'understanding' as 'making sense' of something that makes sense for the objects of the enquiry; more specifically, as making sense of human affairs, manifestations, actions, creations, institutions, and so forth. In all such cases 'making sense' includes interpretation.

The genre under scrutiny is that of social science. It is not the interpretation of perennial works of art or works of philosophy that we are discussing. Our sole focus here is the understanding of a language game that claims to be scientific and objective. Neither the arts nor philosophy take pride in their 'objectivity', a term that, at least in philosophy, is suspected of eclecticism. Yet objectivity is one of the major norms in the social sciences. It is the norm of justice in the social sciences. Just as one must be just to make the right decision, one must be objective to obtain true knowledge. But how can the commitment to objectivity be maintained, given that true knowledge relies upon, and derives from, true understanding, and yet every understanding involves misunderstanding?

Let me refer to a point made earlier: true knowledge in social sciences cannot be deduced from the ultimate principles of reason or gained from observation, experiment or introspection. Social science extracts meaning from the meaningful – for example, the testimonies of witnesses to an event, testimonies of the participant members of a way of life, whether these people are alive or dead, or testimonies written about testimonies, or about objectivations of any kind. Objectivity requires that all available witnesses be given a hearing if their testimony is relevant to the issue under enquiry. Moreover, they should be given equal attention (a 'fair hearing'). No social scientist can decide in advance which testimony he or she will give credence to. Only after having heard all these testimonies, after having understood and compared them, will the scientist give more credence to one testimony than to another.

Reading testimonies is the most complex task in social science. This is not because reading in itself is a more demanding task than interpreting a unique work of art or a philosophical opus, but because this particular task involves a great variety of different types of reading. One must learn to read straightforward narratives, reports, statistical material, semi-fictitious stories and previous interpretations, just as one must learn to listen 'understandingly' to oral testimonies, penetrate to the hidden meaning of visual testimonies such as artefacts, whether of a ceremonial or practical nature, and do many other things besides. Certain social sciences also require the interpretation of the effective history (*Wirkungsgeschichte*) of an historical event, an institution, an idea, and so on.[11] The best relationship to such a witness is not one of interrogation but one of conversation; in other words, the hermeneutic model of interpretative activity. Understanding is deepest if both persons communicate on equal terms, if both can ask questions, and if the Gadamerian 'fusion of horizons' comes about. However, a deep understanding of this type in the social sciences is not always adequate to its task. Communicative *qua* conversational reading can produce the best level of understanding of all approaches. But then it cannot offer certain kinds of understanding where conversational communication is intrinsically 'off limits'. For example, the reading of statistics is a work of interpretation, but it neither requires nor permits conversational communication. It does not aim at mutual understanding and cannot result in the fusion of horizons.

Conclusive hermeneutic literature frequently offers us general formulas for proper interpretation.[12] Among other things, we are told that interpretation should not aim at discovering what *a* single person (or even a group of persons) means to do when doing this or that. What we must discover is rather the meaning of the action of the 'imaginary institution', the objectivation itself. This formula is based on the experience everyone is familiar with from simple introspection: the meaning of what we have done is frequently not identical with, or tantamount to, what we have meant to do. And the more important an action or choice, the more this is so. Were it otherwise, we could not and would not reinterpret our own life, our own decisive choices, in so many different ways.

So far I have listed certain fundamental criteria of objective (just) interpretation in social science. If someone has questioned the available and relevant witnesses and has tried hard to discover what they have really meant, irrespective of whether this testimony is reliable or unreliable; if the social scientists has given hearing to those witnesses whose testimonies are unfriendly to this scientist's initial position, value commitment, theory, and the like; if this social scientist has entered into communication in the form of symmetric reciprocity with every witness who was ready to enter into a communication of this kind – if all these things have been done, then the interpretation will have exhausted every criterion of objectivity and thus of scientificity. As we shall see, such an interpretation will still involve misinterpretation, but it will not *be* misinterpretation.

A work can be termed a 'work of social science' if it has been successful in the quest for objectivity. But not every work of social science is a good, a crucial, an important, or even an interesting work. This statement is more than a truism. It also poses a dilemma. Objectivity requires communicating with and questioning the *relevant* witnesses. But who are these witnesses? It is easy to see that the quest for objectivity may end in the questioning of improper as well as proper witnesses, may see a reluctance to criticize the testimony of this or that witness, and even a poor ability to distinguish between reliable and unreliable witnesses. To effect a proper selection among the witnesses, to dismiss some of them while calling up others not yet considered likely candidates, to have the courage to neglect certain testimonies by giving good reasons for their being neglected, to give credence to other testimonies by listing good reasons why they deserve to be given credence – all these are criteria of a good, innovative, ingenious, insightful, or beautiful interpretation. One needs a good theory to be able to interpret in this manner. Koselleck mentions *Theoriebedurftigkeit* in social inquiry.[13] This is an apt term, for interpretation longs, so to speak, for a theory.

Normally, theory in social sciences is double-edged. There is a higher theory, which provides the most general evaluative and speculative perspective in the quest for meaning. Without a preliminary hypothesis, without a general set of contexts of meaning, no quest for meaning can occur. A higher theory of this kind can be borrowed from a particular philosophy. After the higher (general) theory has provided the framework of selection and has predetermined the main topic of conversation with the witnesses, the final version of the theory is presented. The latter may be an 'applied theory', such as a theory of a single historical event, of a concrete institution, of a particular ceremony or of a particular tribe; that is, it may be a theory of something singular, whether synchronic or dyachronic. Yet it may also be the reconfirmation of the initial theory as social theory (a unity of philosophy and social science).[14]

Whether higher or applied, theory always explains. Explanation can be nomothetic. Nevertheless, explaining single or particular events, institutions, actions and cultural patterns by subjecting these things to general laws is but one particular kind of explanation. Hempel's contention that explanation must include at least one general law cannot be realized in the social sciences.[15] If this contention were accepted, we would be forced to usher out some of the greatest classical texts of this genre (among them, Weber's *Protestant Ethic*), as well as some of the best contemporary works. The other extreme, that of banning general laws from social science, fares no better, especially if we include all monocausal explanations and applications of generalized sentences in this ban (in which case Marx, Durkheim, Toynbee, Foucault and Luhmann would be blacklisted). In short, there are several types of explanations, each belonging to one of three clusters: explanation with efficient causes, explanation with final causes (*causa finalis*), and explanation with formal causes (*causa formalis*). Explanation with efficient causes can take the form of general laws (if X is the case, Y is always and necessarily the case; X is the case, this is why Y is the case), and can also utilize single causes of non-human character – epidemics, plagues – as explanatory devices. However, the most usual form is that of multicausal explanation, where all causes are 'efficient causes', or only one of them is such. Explanation with final causes is sometimes – though illegitimately – regarded as interpretation. Weber's ideal types were conceived as devices of an explanation of this kind. The ideal type is a marionette actor who is not to be interpreted, although is construed after certain texts have already been interpreted. Institutions are then explained by the 'ends–means' rationality attributed to the puppet. Goffmann no longer interprets his puppets at all.[16] As Ricoeur correctly remarked, the structuralist textual explication of Levi-Strauss is explanatory, and not interpretative.[17] In most cases, social science combines at least two different kinds of explanation and interpretation.

Explanation is the brain of social science; interpretation is its soul. Finding the proper balance between explanation and interpretation is a matter of *phronesis* to the same degree as finding the right proportion between the 'core' and the 'ring' or finding the relation of the proper *kind* of interpretation adequate to the sub-genre, to the issue under scrutiny. The proper balance must be achieved anew each time and on every occasion; there is no universal formula, no metamethod, no general guideline to apply.

For the third time now I have emphasized the mobilization of *phronesis*, the role played by prudential judgement in the social sciences. However, prudential judgement alone does not vouchsafe distinction. For the latter to be achieved, imagination is also required. Imagination without good judgement yields dilettantish results, whereas good judgement without imagination yields a thoroughly professional result but adds almost nothing important to the self-knowledge of society. Michael Polanyi remarked that there is always somthing new in every interpretation.[18] This is correct, but the new can still be of little significance. And all the same, there is not always something new in explanation. Within a school of thought, interpretations may vary just as the topics addressed may vary, but the general framework remains the same. Creative imagination opens new theoretical horizons in inventing new explanatory frameworks, in rearranging previous theories, cultural traditions and interpreted facts from a new perspective, from a new, or at least extensively reinterpreted, paradigm. Out of a new horizon, texts are read in a new light and are extensively reinterpreted. New dimensions of the text are opened up for reading from this new perspective, while others are closed or simply forgotten. It is at this point that it becomes clear why every interpretation also involves misinterpretaiton.

One can affirm with Lukács that certain texts are intensively infinite. In respect of intensive infinitude, a text can be reread on an infinite number of occasions such that every new reading will differ from every previous one *without* the introduction of an explanatory framework of any kind. Representative works of art and philosophy can justly be characterized as 'intensive infinitudes'. As a rule the social sciences do not read texts of intensive infinitude, though this is not excluded either. Other types of texts do not constitute a world of their own, and this is precisely why they are not intensively infinite, but it is also why their proper reading requires an explanatory framework or perspective. Read from one or another theoretical perspective, the text will be illuminated from these different aspects. The illumination coming from one particular perspective will vanish when the text is explored from another perspective. Zande witchcraft, as described by Levy-Bruhl,[19] has since been interpreted and reinterpreted several times. This phenomenon almost served as a training ground for different theories, all of them agreeing about *what* the Zande do and what kind of beliefs they attach to what they are doing (this is the core of the argument), yet each of them explaining these practices in terms different from all others. This is why each theory emphasizes one unique aspect of these practices and beliefs, and this is why each theory draws different conclusions from the analysis. On my part, I find some of the interpretations equally plausible (that is, true) and equally objective. For me, these are fair, objective and good interpretations of the same practices and beliefs from the perspective of one or another theory. The theories (and the interpretations) are alternative in character, that is, they may contain conflicting, even irreconcilable, statements or interpretations. Thus each interpretation perforce involves misinterpretation as well. This simple example stands for similar alternatives in all the social sciences and in more complex cases. However, since interpretation has been made 'pluralistic' by different theoretical–explanatory frameworks, I cannot but reaffirm my initial position and hypothesis: in social science, every understanding involves misunderstanding. Yet it should be borne in mind that the criteria of understanding in the social sciences are not identical with those in philosophy. Social sciences are open to falsification, whereas philosophies are not. Consequently, despite the non-cumulative propensity of social sciences, certain interpretations or theories of the genre can be dismissed for good once their fundamental statements have been falsified, even if they have lived up to the criteria of 'objectivity'.

V

Zygmunt Baumann, relying heavily on Habermas's consensus theory, has made the interesting statement that truth in sociology consists of the agreement between the researcher and the object of his or her research (the participant members).[20] Because I have already made the theoretical recommendation that social sciences aim at true knowledge, and *not* at Truth, I will discuss Baumann's claim but will substitute the term 'true knowledge' for the concept of 'truth'.

As already mentioned, the language of enquiry and that of the presentation must be fully translatable into the language of the participant members of the institution under enquiry and vice versa, for without the fulfilment of this criterion communication as mutual understanding is not possible. The condition of a possible consensus is not yet consensus. Moreover, consensus is much too vague a concept in this context: we must ask the question, 'consensus *on what?*' People can agree with the social scientist that 'this is' what they are actually doing, actually saying or really believe, and still disagree concerning the merit, the meaning, and so on of all those issues (with the social scientist or among each other). Extreme examples sometimes illustrate the less extreme cases as well: can a sociological study of a racist group be considered true only under the condition that the researcher and the researched arrive at a complete consensus? If the answer is in the affirmative, only fellow racists of the same 'race' could provide us with a true sociological study of the group, and for reasons of principle. The social scientist can accept the norm of the ideal speech situation, and on his part can conduct the conversation as if this norm were constitutive. Yet because the object of enquiry is the sphere of objective spirit, where the norm of the ideal speech situation is counterfactual, social science must either resign the quest for true knowledge, as long as the above-mentioned norm is counterfactual, or else it must accept the limitation on its claim to consensus.

At this point, I should ask myself whether I have not simply side-stepped certain unpleasant facts in order to avoid unpleasant results. Let us suppose for a moment that only a racist (of the same race) can really understand racist groups, and that this is the condition of reaching full consensus. Of course, it depends on our own understanding of 'understanding' whether we accept this conclusion. Yet it stands to reason that, if we subscribed to the particular notion of understanding that requires the reaching of agreement on issues that presuppose the fusion of the visions of the world, then almost every branch of social science (and first and foremost anthropology) would be disqualified as a medium for reaching understanding.

One argument still remains. All our problems have arisen from the assumption that social scientists enter the enquiry from the standpoint of certain values – so the argument reads. Total value-freedom goes with indifference toward the values under enquiry. Thus if we were to subscribe to total value-freedom, the lack of shared values would not create obstacles to reaching a consensus on facts and meanings. But even if complete value-freedom were possible, and it is not, an approach like this would aggravate our problem rather than simplify it, let alone eliminate it or solve it. If the members of the target group are guided by values, and make claims to these values, whereas the researcher remains at a value-free distance, then even the possibility of communication and mutual understanding (not that of consensus) is out of reach. Apel rightly remarked that without normative engagement not even goal-rational action can be understood.[21]

To summarize, if there are certain shared values, if communication is made possible by translation and the mutual readiness for such an understanding, then a fair consensus between the researcher or researchers and the participant members of the enquiry can indeed come about. Consensus is not the criterion of true knowledge, but if the previous conditions are really met, consensus will be based on, and result from, true knowledge.

At this point I wish to return briefly to Baumann's thesis, in which such an agreement was referred to as truth.[22] I have protested against this formulation, but now I would say that it can be Truth. True knowledge is objective, though relative. Truth is *also* subjective, though absolute. If a particular kind of knowledge provided by social science impacts upon the very existence of a person or a human group, if this person or group recognizes something in this 'true knowledge' that has an essential bearing on their lives, prospects, hopes, fears, experiences, daily practices, choices, and the like, if a work of social science opens up new horizons, new expectations, if it illuminates depths hitherto unknown, unexplored and obscure, if it makes men and women perceive something they have not yet perceived so far, if it elevates them or humiliates them, if it changes their lives – then, and only then, will it reveal *Truth* for them (and will it remain true knowledge, *not* Truth, for others). Yet the fusion of the existential experience of persons (or groups of persons) on the one hand, and of the true knowledge attained by the work of sciences on the other hand, cannot be termed 'consensus'. A more appropriate term would be 'revelation' (even 'mutual revelation'). But revelation is not pursued in the social sciences.

I have now discussed the possibility of consensus between the researcher and the researched. But what about the consensus among social scientists? Is such a consensus possible? Is it desirable?

Social scientists normally claim to have read the relevant texts in the right way, and to have questioned the witnesses conscientiously; they usually claim to have made a proper and objective judgement, to have properly arranged the interpreted facts and 'meanings as quasi-facts', and they say that their explanation of the event, the structure, or the action under enquiry is right. Their claim to 'true knowledge' is based on all these factors. Yet it happens very rarely that social scientists, whether they are committed to nomothetic explanation or pure interpretation, would claim that everyone should consent to everything they have committed to paper. More often than not, an attitude like this indicates delusions of grandeur rather than a genuine scientific claim. This is so for at least two, and sometimes three, reasons. The first reason is obvious. Social scientists themselves, including the most innovative of them, distinguish between the primary and secondary aspects of their recommendations. Agreement on the former is the consensus they seek, whereas the secondary aspects are normally left open to modification. Secondly, the less relativist a social scientist is, the more this person believes in progress in science. Precisely as a result of this creed, this person expects some of his or her own results to be at least further elaborated on, improved, perfected in the future. Conversely, the more relativist a social scientist is, the less vigorous is his or her claim of having provided the only plausible (true) explanation or interpretation. Lastly, social scientists can be perspectivists, with or without being relativist. For example, Marx was a perspectivist in so far as he attributed the elaboration of *the* true theory to the class position of the proletariat, though he was not a relativist. If, however, a special position must be adopted to elaborate the correct theoretical outlook, then obviously a general consensus cannot be reached, for scientists with a 'bourgeois' perspective could not possibly subscribe to the correctness of the explanation of capitalist society provided from a proletarian perspective.

Furthermore, the output of the social sciences comprises texts that can be read and interpreted in different and sometimes completely diverging ways. The more important the text, the more decisive are the unintended inconsistencies within the theory for subsequent interpretations. Accordingly, even if a hundred social scientists agreed that Theory X is true, almost every one of them would give a different account of the theory by emphasizing one aspect rather than another, by viewing it from a variety of perspectives, by dismissing certain of its tenets as insignificant, and so on. Pluralism of interpretation can produce a host of 'neo-prefixes': these days we have neo-Marxists, neo-Ricardians, neo-Weberians, neo-Durkheimians, and sometimes a mixture of all of them. Hence, even if there is a consensus that 'Theory

X is true and right', there is absolutely no consensus as to *what* Theory X is essentially all about, no consensus as to *what* Theory X really means. One could reply to this that, despite this obvious pluralism, a residual Schleiermacher is hidden in the minds of all interpreters in so far as they all cherish the belief that finally, after every interpretative possibility has been exhausted or combined or corrected, we shall arrive at the only true and authentic, in other words the orthodox, interpretation, at which point the enquiry will close. Hirsch has made the interesting observation that the perspectivist usage of such terms as standpoint, attitude and viewpoint are first recorded in the Oxford Dictionary in the mid-nineteenth century.[23] This was also the stage of the final takeoff of the social sciences. But it took an entire century – a century that bore witness to the emergence of the sociology of knowledge and the conquests made by anthropology – to exorcise this residual Schleiermacher from the interpreters' minds. It seems as if today there is only one consensus: the consensus that no consensus exists in the social sciences. It is unnecessary to enumerate all the (interpreted) facts on which this 'consensus on non-consensus' is based. They include differences of culture, of values, of group perspectives, of biographies; the infinite possibilities of arranging interpreted 'meanings as quasi-facts' in theories; the idiosyncracies of particular paradigms; and the fact that the topic under enquiry cannot be same, just the identity of identity and non-identity. Without chasing paradoxical formulations, one could add one more item: that there is not even consensus on the impossibility of consensus in the social sciences, because the phrase 'lack of consensus' is just as vague a notion as the term 'consensus'. A lack of *what kind* of consensus, a lack of consensus *on what* – these are the questions left wide open.

To subscribe to the thesis that there is no consensus at all in social theory, and that any attempt at consensus is futile, and would finally be recognized as hopeless, is nothing more than a claim of *total* relativism. It has often been noted that total relativism is self-contradictory. Hirsch's *aperçu* is worth being quoted: 'I was one told by a theorist who denied the possibility of correct interpretation that I had not interpreted his writings correctly.' This anecdote goes deeper than it appears to. One simply cannot participate in the language game of social science and simultaneously subscribe to total relativism. Because the genre excludes fiction by having a referent, or referents, outside the text (for example another text), it must proceed *as if* true knowledge can be achieved, even if the author does not believe that it can be achieved. Here we are confronted with a case where subjective meaning and objective meaning do not coincide. Subjectively, the author can be a total relativist, but his or her writings cannot be totally relativistic in character as long as he or she operates within the framework of social science and does not write fiction. If you have referents outside the text, others can and will turn to the same referent, and they will assess your text not (or not only) in terms of beauty, perfection, wit, elegance, but – alas – also in terms of right and wrong, true and untrue, even more or less true ('there is some truth in it', or 'it is pure fantasy'), and the like. As long as the text of the total relativist remains a text of social science, this text has just as much right to a 'correct' interpretation as all other texts have.

If we imagine a social scientist who remains within the genre of social science, who is not a subscriber to total relativism but a subscriber to perspectivism, and who believes that most relativist arguments are relevant, we have a position that can be termed restricted (or limited) relativism. Restricted (or limited) relativism does not entail the rejection of the ideas (norms) of social science, including those of verisimilitude and the quest for objectivity. It does not mean that none of the explanations or interpretations is true, nor does it mean that all of them are equally true. It advises us that there can be more than one good theory about the same social phenomenon, that sometimes many theories can be true, and equally so. Yet it does not follow from this position of restricted (limited) relativism that 'anything goes': many things do go, but not everything does. Let me refer back to my earlier discussion: every interpretation involves misinterpretation, every understanding involves misunderstanding. But *not* every misinterpretation is an interpretation (of the referent), and not every misunderstanding is understanding.

So what kind of consensus can in fact be claimed? Social scientists, in so far as they play the game according to the rules, the norms of the genre, have the right to procedural–formal consensus. Their fellow social scientists must agree, they claim, that they have sought true knowledge, that they have made the necessary effort to live up to the norm of objectivity. This recognition is an obvious right of all those having fulfilled an obligation (of playing the game according to the rules). On the other hand, the social scientist does not have the right to a substantive consensus. And yet it is exactly such a substantive consensus (agreement upon *what* the particular scientist asserted) that is more often than not claimed. The right to a substantive consensus is therefore a claim to an 'imperfect right'. Perfect rights go with obligations, imperfect rights go with accomplishments. (An example of this is the right to the preconditions for developing our personal talents.) The claim to substantive consensus (based on the imperfect right) is redeemed if others agree that the theory and the interpretation are one of the good, right and plausible theories and interpretations among many, although these others need not always be fellow scientists. Recognition of the claim to substantive consensus can be the case even if the agreeing 'others' criticize the theory or the interpretation after accepting them as fundamentally true.

The claim to formal consensus can be criticized; it can also be rejected on the grounds of foul play. This latter action usually occurs through the use of the device of 'unmasking': the theory is exposed as a covert or overt expression of a particularistic interest, the will to power, or an unconscious wish. However, the process of 'unmasking', illuminating as it might be, does not yet prove that 'foul play' is the case, nor does it in itself justify the withholding of procedural–formal consensus. The act of 'unmasking' legitimately results in the withholding of formal consensus if, and only if, it can be proved that the prejudgement of the author has hardened into prejudice, that the quest for objectivity was never authentic in that the author selected only those witnesses whose testimonies fitted his or her preconceived purpose, that well-known and credible testimonies were neglected, that the author proceeded in a strongly rhetorical manner. It was in this way that Vidal-Naquet argued for the withholding of formal consensus (and even a minimum of procedural recognition) from Faurisson's writings.[24] If the claim to formal consensus is disclaimed, simultaneously a general consensus for the disclaimer is also claimed (everyone who plays fair should reject foul play). 'Unmasking' can also denote the process of disclaiming claims for substantive consensus alone. But here one cannot claim a general consensus for the disclaimer because one must accept that the theory will be regarded as true by those who share the perspective of the theorist – his interests, unconscious impulses or other typical motivations. Yet the claim for substantive consensus can be criticized on several other grounds, all of which finally boil down to the issue of 'lack of accomplishment' (insufficient degree of *phronesis*, inattentive or inaccurate observation, faulty imagination).

The third mode of eliminating theories from among the 'true ones' is also relative. Although social sciences are not cumulative in the sense of problem-solving, cumulative knowledge can be found within the framework of these sciences. Previously unknown documents can be discovered, additional information can be gathered, even certain events can occur that make particular aspects of an earlier work of social science obsolescent without rendering the theory as a whole obsolescent. In this way certain tenets of a theory can be falsified, though it is also the case that we simply reach back to an 'old' theory for inspiration and add that this or that statement of the theory is no longer valid. It can legitimately be said of a particular work of social science that it is 'excellent, it is truly innovative, but here the author is wrong', or 'on this point the author is right but on this other point she is wrong': in fact, almost all book reviews are written along such lines. So without much reflection we certainly accept that there are different theories about the same issue, problem or action that are yet equally true, just as we accept that there exists a cluster of theories about the same issue, problem or action that are regarded as basically true by some but only as 'containing certain true elements' by others.

Formal consensus is the consensus of a broadly defined scientific community. Entry into this community is free, but the community at large has the right to determine the conditions of both acknowledgement and of non-recognition. A person can claim complete formal consensus (can claim to have avoided foul play). Substantive consensus is however settled not within the scientific community but, in the last instance, by everyone who attempts to elucidate social and political matters for whatever reason – either to translate into action, to illuminate the conditions of his or her life, or out of sheer curiosity. Consensus is achieved if everyone familiar with the propositions of the theory, and certain criticisms thereof, can say, 'there is truth in it', 'there are true elements in it', and so on. To my mind this can be regarded as *the* ideal consensus in social science. If only non-professionals find truth in a theory while social scientists find none at all, or, conversely, if only social scientists find the 'true aspect' in it whereas interested and committed citizens do not, this theory is not true and can be thrown into the bin. A greater, deeper or more complete consensus cannot be sought, but can only be forced or imposed upon someone in a pluralistic cultural and social universe.

VI

This exercise in the hermeneutics of social science was introduced with a fragment of a general theory of history, or, to use a fashionable misnomer, by a fragmented metanarrative. I have presented the idea that modern social science, whether nomothetic or hermeneutic, makes an attempt, or rather the attempt, at transcending both the possibilities and the limitations of modern historical consciousness. Modern men and women who have forsaken the certitude of a perennial Truth have not thereby foresaken the quest for certitude. The quest for knowledge as social science was to provide such a certitude. Science could not have become the dominating world-view of modernity had people not vested their quest for certitude in everything 'scientific'. Even now, in an age of sweeping relativism, the term 'scientific' for the ordinary language user means being certain, being beyond doubt, being true.

Have the social sciences lived up to their promises? Have they delivered the goods, or, for that matter, have they delivered any goods? Is this bastard offspring of philosophy, science and ideology (for the metaphorical parentage in this case is not restricted to two parents) not a misunderstanding as it stands?

Roughly half a century ago Freud characterized religion as an 'illusion', a wish-fulfilment, though he attributed what he termed 'historical Truth' to this illusion. In doing so he raised the rhetorical question of whether science will come to be regarded as yet another illusion alias a wish-fulfilment, a medium conveying yet another, a modern 'historical Truth'.[25] This question was rhetorical, for Freud immediately answered it in the negative. Science can err, but it is no illusion because it presents grounds for its claims. There is no court of appeal higher than the court of reason, and it is precisely this court of appeal that science recognizes. Total cultural relativism answers Freud's (rhetorical) question in the affirmative. The sciences, and among them the social sciences, are invented and committed to paper as the myths of modernity, and have no special claims in relation to any other myth. Limited cultural relativism, however, cannot follow in the footsteps of either the first or the second answer.

To a certain degree *all* cultural products are wish-fulfilments, yet this does not determine the character of such products. Their meaning, their truth content, does not depend on their being a wish-fulfilment. I have not denied but rather emphasized that modern social science also serves as 'wish-fulfilment'. Furthermore, I would unhesitatingly subscribe to Freud's contention that religions do too. Yet it does not follow from this that either religions or the sciences (including the social sciences) are either 'illusions' or delusions. Nor does it follow that they are alike, or even that their claims are similar or redeemable in the same manner.

Also absolute relativism is wish-fulfilment of a kind: the wish in question is a death wish. Products of Western culture turn against their own traditions and develop suicidal inclinations. Absolute cultural relativists wish to unmake, to undo, the modern Western differentiation of cultural spheres. And because this differentiation includes the emergence in our ways of life of the discursive mode called rationalism, in politics as well as in the sciences, the death wish turns against the author of rational discourse, namely against the individual who thinks with his or her own mind.

Before returning to the initial question of whether the social sciences have lived up to their promises, whether they have delivered the goods, or any goods for that matter, let me briefly summarize the results of the above detour. Social science is not an illusion, although it is a wish-fulfilment. At the same time, it is a dubious kind of wish-fulfilment, for out of this has sprung the death wish.

Social science has promised certitude and self-knowledge as the result of a new, rationalist quest for meaning. This promise has not been kept. Where there was certainty, there was neither meaning nor self-knowledge; where there was meaning and self-knowledge, there was no certainty. The quest for meaning and self-knowledge that was combined with the quest for certainty in the great narratives of Marx, Durkheim, Freud and others, has ended in resignation. The 'bid for certainty' has been abandoned. What was initially seen as 'taking hold' of necessity has ended up in the consciousness of contingency. Viewed from this general narrative, the 'death wish' is the same wish as that which was supposed to be fulfilled by social science in the first place. It expresses the sentiment that the initial wish has not been fulfilled, that the promise has not been kept, and that because of this social science itself is but a misunderstanding. Yet is it?

The contemporary individual is aware of his or her contingency, but is unhappy in this awareness. Yet because we today are aware of our contingency, an apocalyptic tone does not suit us. There is something of the buffoon in the contingent person who makes statements about the 'end of', about 'the last'; a prophet who disclaims or precludes any certainty with his first gesture is by definition a false prophet. Granted this, a person aware of his or her contingency can still try to transform this contingency into his or her destiny. To my mind, this path is still open for our own culture.

On one count at least, the social sciences have not failed; they have indeed provided self-knowledge, and they never ceased providing self-knowledge of modern society, of a contingent society, of one society among many, our society. The social sciences can never provide a type of knowledge that is 'certain', for no self-knowledge is ever certain, and yet they provide knowledge of a kind one can go by, if one makes an attempt at transforming our contingency into our destiny. Western modernity is our contingency. Instead of destroying it, we could try to transform it into our destiny. This statement sounds odd, though at heart it conveys a simple enough message. An individual has transformed his or her contingency into his or her destiny if this person has arrived at the consciousness of having made the *best* out of his or her practically infinite possibilities. A society has transformed its contingency into its destiny if the members of this society arrive at the awareness that they would prefer to live at no other place and at no other time than the here and now. And it is only modern society that can transform its contingency into its destiny, because it is only now that we have arrived at the consciousness of contingency. The sphere of social science can provide contemporary actors with the meaningful and true knowledge that is indispensable for such a project to be devised and executed. Certainty we can still seek it, in metaphysics, art, religion and human attachment, and sometimes we even find it in these pursuits. But social science will not promise us certainty; instead it will set us free. One need not subscribe to the great narrative of the Hegelian philosophy of history to arrive at its conclusion: here is Rhodus, here you jump.

Notes

1 G. W. F. Hegel, *Lectures on Philosophy of History*, Introduction.
2 Max Weber, 'Science as a vocation', in Gerth and Mills's collection of Weber's writings (Philadelphia: Fortress Press, 1965).
3 Anthony Giddens, *The Constitution of Society* (Cambridge: Polity Press, 1984).
4 R. G. Collingwood, *The Idea of History* (Oxford, Clarendon Press, 1962).
5 Jürgen Habermas, *The Theory of Communicative Action* (Boston, Beacon Press, 1985, 1987).
6 Richard Rorty, *Consequences of Pragmatism* (University of Minnesota Press, 1982).
7 Alfred Schutz, *Phenomenology of Social World* (Evanston: Northwestern University Press, 1967).
8 George Lukács, *Heidelberger Asthetik* (Darmstadt-Neuwied: Luchterhand, 1974), and *Heidelberg Philosophie der Kunst* (Darmstadt-Neuwied: Luchterhand, 1974).
9 H. G. Gadamer, *Philosophical Hermeneutics* (Berkeley: University of California Press, 1977).

42   *Hermeneutics of Social Science*

10   Alasdair MacIntyre, 'Is understanding religion compatible with believing?' in *Rationality*, ed. B. R. Wilson (Oxford: Blackwell, 1974).
11   H. G. Gadamer, *Truth and Method* (New York: Seabury Press, 1975).
12   Among others, the following books discuss this and related matters: R. J. Bernstein, *Beyond Objectivism and Relativism* (Philadelphia: University of Pennsylvania Press, 1983); J. Bleicher, *The Hermeneutic Imagination* (London: Routledge & Kegan Paul, 1982); C. Castoriadis, *Domaines de l'homme* (Paris: Editions du Seuil, 1986); F. R. Dallmayr, *Twilight of Subjectivity* (Amherst: University of Massachusetts Press, 1981); C. Taylor, *The Explanation of Behavior* (New York: Humanities Press, 1964); G. H. Van Wright, *Explanation and Understanding* (Ithaca: Cornell University Press, 1971); and Peter Winch, 'The idea of a social science' and 'Understanding a primitive society', in *Rationality*, ed. B. R. Wilson (Oxford: Blackwell, 1974).
13   R. Koselleck, *Critique and Crisis* (Cambridge: MIT Press, 1988).
14   Agnes Heller, *A Theory of History* (London: Routledge & Kegan Paul, 1982).
15   Carl G. Hempel, *Aspects of Scientific Explanation* (New York: Free Press, 1965).
16   Erving Goffmann, *Presentation of the Self in Everyday Life* (Garden City, N.Y.: Doubleday, 1959).
17   Paul Ricoeur, *Hermeneutics and the Moral Sciences*, ed. J. B. Thompson (Cambridge: Cambridge University Press, 1981).
18   Michael Polanyi, *Personal Knowledge* (New York: Harper Torch Books, 1958).
19   E. E. Evans-Pritchard, *Zande Trickster* (Oxford: Clarendon, 1967).
20   Z. Baumann, *Hermeneutics and Social Science* (London: Hutchinson, 1978).
21   K. O. Apel, *Transformation der Philosophie*, I–II (Frankfurt-Main: Suhrkamp-Verlag, 1976).
22   Z. Baumann, *Hermeneutics and Social Science*.
23   E. D. Hirsch, Jr, *The Aims of Interpretation* (Chicago: The University of Chicago Press, 1976).
24   P. Vidal-Naquet, *Les Assassins de la mémoire* (Paris: Edition la Decouverte, 1987).
25   Sigmund Freud, *The Future of an Illusion*, in S. Freud, *Civilization, Society and Religion* (Harmondsworth: Penguin, 1985).

2
Can Everyday Life be Endangered?

I

Everyday life has attracted scant attention in its own right in the philosophical tradition of the past two and a half thousand years. However, it has attained the rank of a problem worthy of philosophical and sociological examination in the twentieth century. The problem may be addressed within various paradigms, each of which generates its own vocabulary. One particular paradigm discusses 'everyday life', another 'life' pure and simple, the third 'life-world', yet another again 'natural attitude' or 'ordinary language', etc. Some of them mention 'inauthentic life' of *'das Mann'*, while others speak of basic traditions, or 'workaday life', *quotidienneté* and much else. It is not as though they were all discussing the same *thing*, however, because everyday life itself is not 'some/thing' but rather the shared modern life experience on which *our* intersubjective constitution of the world rests. Because of this, all theories and philosophies relying on one of these paradigms of intersubjective world constitution must include the problem of everyday life, our shared experience of intersubjectivity, in their world interpretations. A philosophical paradigm is understood as the vision of an author or several authors. All of those who share in this vision will find it easy to accept the paradigm, and thus the world interpretation, of a philosophy expressing this particular vision. For those who do not share this paradigm, the interpretation, while perhaps comprehensible, will seem implausible. If this sceptic is also a philosopher, he or she will certainly find the proper means to put to the test and question the veracity of that particular world interpretation.

This is not to suggest that all visions are equal in terms of their breadth, veracity, seriousness and relevance. It suggests only that visions that would be regarded as equally plausible by an astronaut, the 'metaobserver', were he or she in possession of an objective measure to appraise world interpretations growing out of life experiences, could be accepted as self-evident by men and women who share certain life experiences while being rejected by others who do not share these same life experiences. By life experiences I certainly do not mean to refer merely to acts, events and happenings, but also to general frameworks of meanings, world-views and institutions of signification which guide, synthesize and order the process of experiencing itself.

The problem discussed here ('whether everyday life can be endangered, and if so, to what extent and by what') has been addressed within the framework of a large number of paradigms. I will address the problem within my own framework, which encompasses the vision of my own life experiences, and which I also share with others. The predictable objection, namely that I should have worked with another paradigm, is a fairly irrelevant one. For after the spectacular collapse of the self-confident progressivist-modern creed of the nineteenth century, it is about time to dismiss the old Hegelian narrative about 'progress in philosophy'. Unless we hold that everything that has ever been asserted about general principles of Being is now encompassed in the totality of concrete universality, we must give up the pretence that one particular paradigm is, by definition, the only relevant one, and that it provides authority for looking down condescendingly at other paradigms which are not yet on the level of the latest discovery. Nowadays, the paradigm of language and its sub-paradigms are guilty of 'philosophical imperialism'. The theses that 'every/thing' is language or 'every/thing' is communication are all equally and absolutely legitimate philosophical speculations. But so are the paradigms of work, imagination and consciousness – and, indeed, the proposition that everything is matter and form is not inferior to them. And here I have limited myself to those paradigms that, one way or another, make a case for what I have termed 'the intersubjective constitution of reality'.

My paradigm is one of 'the human condition', a concept I will specify later. However, it should be immediately apparent that the paradigm of 'the human condition' is almost as broad as the absolute spirit, for it encompasses everything that has become the point of reference for all other modern paradigms, such as language, speech, communication, interaction, work, imagination, consciousness, understanding, interpretation and so much else. This is actually why I find the paradigm so relevant, given that everyday life is *all* of these things and that none of them holds an absolute primacy in everyday life itself. The latter point is particularly true if we examine everyday life from the viewpoint of the single person, the individual. The single person is engaged in entirely heterogeneous activities. He or she is, or becomes, a whole person in performing heterogeneous activities. He or she is not 'all language' or 'all consciousness', 'all body', 'all spirit', 'all labouring animal', 'all creative technology', or 'all political activism', etc. Yet he or she is, or can become, all of them. In order to avoid misunderstandings, I would like to stress that taking the standpoint of the individual is far from being tantamount to Cartesianism, methodological individualism or personalism. For 'taking the standpoint of the individual' has neither an ontological nor an epistemological status. It has neither an explanatory nor an interpretative value. And yet it is none the less a standpoint. One can assert that the person is a product of his or her environment and still look at the environment with the eyes of its product. One may also assert that in human life there are things and instances that are far more valuable than the single individual, and still look at those 'far more valuable things' from the viewpoint of the individual. One can, furthermore, assert that men and women always stand in the network of social relations, yet this should not imply that the only network worthy of enquiry is that particular network, or that the constituents of the network are for theoretical purposes non-existent. Individuals exist. Those who nowadays make statements about 'the end of the individual' nevertheless publish books in their own name, and not in the name of some mystical entity called 'Discourse'. The celebrated argument of Diogenes against Zeno made a practical reference to everyday experience; so does mine. In a theory of everyday life this seemingly pedestrian gesture is completely relevant.

II

'The human condition' encompasses everything that all living human beings must share, that dead human beings had shared, that yet unborn human beings will perforce share. In our modern world the human condition resides in everyday life. This is not to say that our whole modern everyday life, as it is, is coextensive with the human condition. Everyday life consists of constant and variable features. The content of everyday life changes quite frequently when compared to the modification of its structure. Furthermore, historians can pinpoint quite a few significant modifications in the structure of everyday life, the most drastic one emerging along the line of demarcation between the modern and the pre-modern. The human condition resides only in the constant features of everyday life. The static and the variable aspects of everyday existence are certainly for all theoretical and practical purposes fully intertwined. Yet it is not simply for the sake of analytical clarity that the line of demarcation between the constant and the variable features (patterns) should be drawn; or even for the seemingly obvious reason to make another attempt at a streamlined 'grand narrative' about the vicissitudes of 'human nature'. For the story of human nature is not identical with the story of the human condition. The former is a broadly designed historical narrative in both its optimistic–progressivist and pessimistic–regressivist versions. These versions read as follows: 'Once upon a time there was a human nature, the narrow limits of which were forced back and broadened by human industry or cooperation'; or, alternatively, 'Once upon a time there was a human nature which has been degraded and transformed into a one-dimensional nullity.'

The story of the human condition is not a story proper. If one tells a story that intends to come close to that of human nature, one tells the story not of the human condition itself, but rather of the historicity that has been conditioned by the human condition. The human condition itself is a category of limit or a limiting category. Since the category encompasses everything that happens to be the minimal condition of human life, if a single aspect of 'the human condition' is missing, there is no human life. The human condition is cosmos in so far as it is human order. The lack of human condition, or any one single constituent thereof, is chaos, doomsday, the very end of (human) life. This being said, the thesis that the human condition resides in the constant features of everyday life in our modern world is laden with serious connotations. And it will become evident that distinguishing between its static and variable features in modern life is important not only for analytical reasons, whether or not they are in fact intertwined. If certain variable features of everyday life vanish, no chaos, no end of human life will come about. If, however, the constant features are endangered, everyday life as such will reach its own limit, the twilight zone between cosmos and chaos.

III

In order to support the thesis that, in modernity, the human condition resides in everyday life, it is necessary first to present my conception of the human condition in a nutshell.

The human condition can, first of all, be determined (*bestimmt*) as substituting social regulation for instinct regulation. Regularity, repetition, repeatability and uniformity are the order of living things. In the animal kingdom instincts take care of this order. In certain species which are closest to our own, learning processes do take place against the backdrop of a less rigid, while still existent instinct regulation. The human infant carries in his or her body/mind a complex order of living things, but the imprints of cooperation, enmity and conflict are not among them. Regularity, repeatability, repetition and uniformity, as patterns of intercourse among living beings, are each given (presented) as an external entity and force for the human infant. As a result of this, learning processes cannot have recourse to the innate patterns alone; they must be mediated by the external order. It is only via the appropriation of the norms and rules of this external order that the infant will open up for further learning processes. The human condition is therefore mediated. The newborn is certainly not like a *tabula rasa*; he or she is also born with a quite unique genetic code. Nothing in this genetic code predetermines him or her for having been born in exactly this and that particular social pattern. Everyone is thrown into a concrete network of social regulations by the accident of birth. Culture takes care of transforming this accident, perceived as organic embeddedness, into fate or providence. Both social regulations and genetic uniqueness are therefore prior to human experience. The social and genetic *a priori* need to be dovetailed for the invariably unique system called 'human being' to come about. Human experiencing takes off in the process of such dovetailing. Human being is the being who has jumped across the abyss or, to use Gehlen's term, who has succeeded in bridging the hiatus. Not every genetic *a priori* fits each and every social *a priori*, and, even if it does, it does not fit to the same degree. In the human being there is a constant tension between the two dovetailed *a priori*. This tension may be strong or weak. However, whether strong or weak, human beings nevertheless live in the midst of this tension. That this tension can be destructive or creative is a fact that I will not discuss here any further.

Human persons are thus created and self-creating systems. They are neither part of nature nor part of society, for they come about via the dovetailing of the social and the genetic *a priori*. The co-temporality and co-spatiality of these two *a priori* is sheer accident.

The human condition is a constant and it is constantly borne in mind. Ever since the emergence of reflective self-consciousness, the puzzle of the human condition has always been addressed in fables, mythologies, religions, philosophies and psychologies. The centre of attention has been the tension itself.

IV

Society needs to provide rules for the acquisition of the means of subsistence, for human cooperation and conflict, and for meaning-constitution. If any of these rules were missing, the process of dovetailing would certainly miscarry. Irrespective of whether such rules are simple, rigid and monotonous, or complex, flexible and highly differentiated, one feature remains constant: all three sets of rules need to be dovetailed. It is common knowledge that socialization results in the appropriation not of the whole of the universe, but rather of a tiny portion of it. The question is, what this tiny portion must entail. In my view, it entails the sufficient amount of patterns to ensure the social life of the person and, simultaneously, the reproduction of the social universe. And this tiny cross-segment of the social universe must be presented to each and every newborn. If, in a hypothetical case, a newborn was presented not with the cross-segment of the social universe, but only with a particular set of rules and regulations, or with no socially regulated patterns at all, social life would break down and chaos would set in. Certain theorists warn about the eventuality of our relapse into barbarism. Since this term is misleading, I will instead employ the anthropologically neutral term 'chaos'.

Of what does the 'cross-segment of society' perforce consist? What is this social *a priori* that must be dovetailed with the genetic *a priori* in order for any single human being to be able to join the great chain of living creatures? What is this social *a priori*, one of the ingredients of a new human soul? I have termed this cross-segment 'the sphere of objectivation in itself'. It is, so to speak, the first sphere of the social universe. Without having stepped into this sphere and thus having become a person of a particular social universe, one cannot step into other spheres. What has been acquired here is the foundation of the person's communicative, cognitive, imaginative, creative and emotive possibilities, which are open to them throughout their whole life at the time and on the (social and geographical) spot where they happened to be born by sheer good or bad luck.

I have termed this sphere one of 'objectivation' with good reason. The sphere confronts the newborn as a mere externality, as the alien, the other, the object. This is not meant as a contribution to the thesis of 'repression'. The world of objects both develops the subject as well as represses some of its impulses. Affects and drives are indeed regulated, but in being regulated they are also provided with objects that give them direction. Furthermore, the term 'objectivation' is not equivalent to 'objective'. It also carries with it the connotation that the 'objective' is manifested, re-cast, re-enacted upon by subjects, that is human beings, 'the adult generations' whose living experiences have already been crystallized in everything 'objective'.

Finally, I have termed this sphere 'in itself', by which I mean 'pre-reflective'. One cannot reflect upon this sphere from the standpoint of this very sphere. Cut off from the other spheres, the sphere of 'objectivation in itself' entails what is self-evident, and taken for granted.

The sphere of 'objectivation in itself' consists of the following: (1) rules and norms of ordinary language and language use; (2) rules and prescriptions for using, handling and manipulating objects, especially man-made objects; and (3) rules and norms of human interaction called customs. The three kinds of norms and rules are intertwined, and they are appropriated as such. One of these norms or rules makes proper sense only within the context of the other two, and vice versa. In appropriating this sphere, the person acquires contextual language use, contextual 'know-what' and 'know-how'; they learn to feel and interpret their feelings cognitively in the proper context, to do the right things, to cope with dangers and threats in an adequate manner, to tell right from wrong, good from bad, friend from foe, and so on.

The sphere of objectivation in itself is the sphere of everyday life, but it is neither coterminous nor coextensive with it. In everyday life we absorb certain values, norms and visions, we perform certain practices and actions, we acquire knowledge. All of these activities originated not in the sphere of objectivation in itself, but in other, higher spheres. This is more so today than it has ever been before but it also must be so irrespective of the historical *hic et nunc*. The coeval existence of at least two different spheres of objectivation is an ontological, and not a historical, condition of human life; it is inherent in the human condition. There is a contradiction between having been thrown into a world by sheer accident on the one hand, and the internalization of an external social sphere as taken-for-granted on the other. Since the tension is felt, the taken-for-grantedness of the sphere of objectivation that is to be internalized needs support and justification. It cannot originate in the very sphere that has to be justified; rather, it must originate in another sphere. The sphere of 'objectivation in itself' provides men and women with *meanings*, as a complex of rules, norms, signs and contextual signification, cross-significations. It is precisely meanings (in the plural) that it provides. What it does not provide, however, is meaning in the singular – the meaning of the whole enterprise, of its very existence, of life and of our own life, of everything that it implies. Viewed from this perspective, the human condition includes and presupposes the very existence of another sphere of signification as its necessary (ontological) constituent. I term this sphere one of 'objectivation for itself'. This is the sphere where meaning is provided. Hegel termed it 'absolute spirit' and greatly narrowed its possible content. The sphere of 'objectivation for itself' comprises all kinds of narratives, mythologies of various provenance, speculations, visual representations of all sorts and much more. The common feature of these constituents is that they all provide life with meaning. They can legitimize the existing order to the same extent that they can question its legitimation.

The sphere of 'objectivation for itself' must offer meaning precisely because meaning (in the singular) cannot be generated in the sphere of 'objectivation in itself'. However, the latter operates as a filter system. In order to pass through the network of the sphere of 'objectivization in itself', the meaningful world-views generated in other spheres must be fitted into the proper order and patterns of the lowest, while at the same time fundamental, sphere. The person who is about to appropriate the meanings of the fundamental sphere, as they are presented by taken-for-granted norms and rules, will also absorb and appropriate the meaning as taken-for-granted. The transcontextual meaning appears in contexts (in the plural), and it can be acquired only by context-related practice and thinking. The sphere of 'objectivation in itself' is the sphere of everyday life, for it translates all kinds of normative, cognitive and practical knowledge into its own contextual language network. It thus literally stands between the persons and the higher (less fundamental) objectivations.

The dovetailing of the two *a priori* is accomplished when the person acquires competence in acting, behaving and generally doing things according to the rules of the fundamental sphere of objectivation.

Since men and women generally acquire this competence, our race consists of rational beings. Men and women can undoubtedly acquire this competence, take the rules for granted and still act as if they were incompetent. In other words: they can also be irrational. Furthermore, men and women can acquire the competence and take the rules for granted, and yet act as if the rules were not binding for them. In this scenario, they would then be evil and still rational. Finally, men and women can acquire the competence in minding the rules, yet still reject the relevance (validity, justice, goodness) of one or another such rule. In other words, they can be rational on the first or second level, for if this were otherwise, all expectations would break down, and our race would not survive. Philosophers, prophets and wise men pondered irrationality as a problem and with good cause. One ponders or reflects on something that one does not understand, that lends itself to a great variety of interpretations or that one wants to change and redress. The fundamental rationality of men and women has never been pondered as a problem, for it did not need to be: it has always been taken for granted.

At the inception of this discussion I raised the point that everyday life has become a problem in the twentieth century. In times when even the 'colonization of everyday life' can be discussed (by Habermas), matters that hitherto had been taken for granted might now become the focus of theoretical scrutiny. We may thus raise the question as to what would happen if the fundamental sphere of objectivation ceased to exist as a result of some systemetic development and if it were instead replaced by other objectivations. I will now provisionally put forth the answer to this question. If this came to pass, the (genetic and social) *a priori* of human existence could not be dovetailed at all, humans would cease to be rational, and ultimately human, beings. I can neither imagine nor conceive of this alternative. But I still owe a theoretical explanation/interpretation of this eventuality.

V

The subject of everyday life is the 'human person as a whole', a term coined by Lukács.[1] The activities one needs to perform are heterogeneous. They do not constitute a system. There is after all no systemic connection between saying 'hello' to one another, cooking a meal, having an argument about family expenditures, riding a bus, making a pass and so much else. But one has to know how these things are done

as well as to do these things occasionally and continuously. Everyday
life requires the mobilization of many human abilities. But it does not
require an extreme refinement of any of them, nor does it require
developing our endowments into special talents. Everyday activities
can be performed spontaneously having once been learned, and they
do not necessitate further attention. A lot has been written on the
patterns of everyday thinking and action from Schutz to ethno-
methodology; space does not allow for discussing them here even
briefly. It should be mentioned, however, that none of these patterns
condemns the subject of everyday life to mere passivity. The human
person as a whole is not a puppet pulled by the strings of custom.
Norms need to be interpreted in ever new contexts, persons need to
take initiatives in unforeseeable situations; they must also cope with
the catastrophes of everyday life. Against the backdrop of mere routine
and quasi-instinctive repetition of a kind, the uniqueness of persons
comes literally into relief.

Although two spheres of objectivation are indispensable for human
life, the third kind is not. This third kind, which I have termed the
sphere of 'objectivation-for-and-in-itself', since it has resulted from the
differentiation of the former two, is the sphere of socio-economic-
political institutions. Institutions establish their own sets of norms and
rules of communication, action and procedures. They can be filled
with potential for further development, as well as proving to be cul-de-
sacs. Where the institutional sphere is dense, institutions behave like
systems within the environment of other systems. Still, their fate,
whether one of unfolding or remission, is not decided in the sphere of
'objectivation-for-and-in-itself' alone. To some extent, the institutional
system is always parasitic on both the fundamental and the highest-
ranking sphere. The fundamental sphere never ceases to be the sphere
of the human condition. There is no human race without this sphere,
but without the 'middle sphere' the human race can still exist. The
highest sphere, the one that provides life with meaning, or with the
consciousness of the lack of meaning, performs the same task in the
service of the institutionalized sphere. It legitimizes this sphere and,
with it, power, domination and misery. The legitimizing function of
the highest sphere becomes quite emphatic in the process of its
entrance into the sphere of institutionalization. This is the process in
which 'rendering meaning' itself becomes institutionalized. And yet,
the sphere of 'objectivation for itself' cannot be fully institutionalized,
for if it were it could not provide the fundamental sphere with
meaning. Nor could it then absorb the cultural surplus that pours into

this sphere as a result of the unaccomplished dovetailing of the two human *a priori*. Needless to say, the institutional sphere shapes the other two without ever being able to assimilate them. In the last instance, it is the sphere of institutions that is parasitic on the other two spheres and not vice versa.

The subject of the sphere of institutions is the specialized subject. One can enter an institution (other than the family) only via specialization. The human being as a whole can specialize in more than one kind of action and work. But it cannot be emphasized enough that it is only the human person as a whole who can be specialized.

Thus each of the three spheres requires a different attitude. The fundamental sphere requires the whole human person, the institutional sphere requires the specialized human person, and the sphere of 'objectivation for itself' requires 'human wholeness', to use a Lukácsian term. One can dwell in this sphere once one is *wholly* absorbed, once one fully abandons oneself to it, once one concentrates all of one's abilities, endowments, emotional dispositions, judgemental powers, etc. on performing something in the higher sphere. When we refer to seers and sages, prophets and saints, trances, ecstasy, inspiration, self-abandon, peak-experience, illumination, intuition, the feeling of 'being carried away', full intellectual concentration, being 'all ears' or 'all attention' – in all these terms, whether our vocabulary is mystical or prosaic, we are invariably interpreting the attitude that has been termed 'human wholeness'. Thus, as there are three spheres, there are three attitudes.

VI

Two main types of the socio-political organization, or, to risk oversimplification, two main types of the division of labour, should be juxtaposed here. Historically, the fundamental sphere, that of 'objectivation in itself', is the sphere in which the division of labour is constituted. It is the content, the character of the norms, the rules and regulations of the fundamental sphere that ranks people within the social hierarchy. Types of access to the institutionalized sphere (and to each institution of this sphere) have their preliminary models in this sphere. Moreover, the types of imagination that are inherent in the sphere of objectivation for itself are also filtered through the various stratified 'layers' of social universe in different ways. The fundamental sphere is also the determining sphere. What does the human condition look like in this model? By accident of birth, a person is thrown not only into a particular time and place but also into a particular system of fundamental ways of life. This dual accident amounts to one determination: this is why I employed the term 'determining sphere'. The genetic *a priori* is dovetailed with a very specific social *a priori*. A person needs to cope with things as a serf copes, as a master copes, as a burgher copes, etc.; moreover, they need to cope with different things. Persons born as males or females have to be dovetailed with entirely different sets of everyday regulations; it is the social *a priori* that creates men and women. The accident of birth is both reconfirmed and negated. The life of a person is predestined in the cradle: the social *a priori* is the master designer, and the person fills in the design with the palette of his or her own life experiences. The modification of the design is not an everyday event. In this model, the human conditon is by definition one of inequality, and thus the condition of the unequal division of life chances and freedom.

The second type of social organization puts the whole onus of the division of labour on the sphere of institutions. Modern societies are closer to this second model than to the first – in fact, this is precisely the meaning of 'modern'. Given that all existing modern societies have grown out of social organizations of the first kind, they cannot be viewed as pure representations of the second model. I will discuss only the model, not its empirically existing versions.

No division of labour or stratification is built into the sphere of 'objectivation in itself' in the second model. Viewed from this aspect, men and women are born equal. The social *a priori* does not pre-determine one's future way of life and the page of the future is in this sense left empty. Viewed from this perspective, men and women are therefore born free. One is still thrown into the world by accident, but this accident will not be one's own destiny. This is the situation I have termed as one of contingency. I distinguish between the accident of birth and contingency. The accident of birth is an ontological category inherent in the human condition. Contingency is a historical category inherent in modern historicity. Contingency reconfirms the accident of birth, that is, our human condition, through the consciousness of our accidental existence. Mythological and religious patterns and narratives are no longer being continuously filtered through the patterns of the fundamental sphere in order to relegate the consciousness of accident to the background. While becoming conscious, the accidental character of our being born precisely here and now is also 'sublated' in the Hegelian sense of the word. It is preserved, since this is the human condition, but it is also negated by the openness of our personal horizon. After all, the situation of contingency puts the marshall's baton of life into the sac of each and every person at the moment of his or her birth. The freedom of contingency is possibility. While, in principle, everything is possible, in fact this is not the case. It is the person's responsibility to transform his or her contingency into his or her destiny, with the alternative being to remain in the limbo of mere possibilities.

The onus of social organization, division of labour and stratification is carried on then by the institutional sphere. The function(s) people perform in an institution, or rather in a variety of institutions, will place them at different levels of stratification as well as endow them with a different degree and type of power, wealth and prestige. That is, the person will be stratified as a *specialized* subject, not as a whole human person. This circumstance may allow for a great variety of combinations. In order to answer the question of whether everyday life can be endangered, we have to briefly explore a few typical combinations.

VII

The institutionalized sphere in the modern world is highly inflated in comparison to the pre-modern condition. If one assumes that there is a system, or there are two systems, which fully include all institutions as their subsystems, swallow them, imprint them and determine the logic of their development and expansion, then, given that persons are stratified according to functions they perform in institutions, our view of the modern world must indeed be fairly gloomy. The more the sphere of 'objectivation in itself' would make all men and women born equal and free, the less opportunity those men and women could have to withstand the crushing power of the dominating system(s). This is the model of negative dialectics. It can also serve as the model of the self-destruction of the human condition once carried to its extreme.

Another possible combination is presented by Habermas, whose presupposition is the dual character of what he terms 'integration':[2] it is at the same time social and systems integration. The model is in accord with the first in so far as systems and systems integration are concerned. But it avoids the gloomy prospects of a negative dialectics by asserting the continual presence of social integration. Simultaneously with the inflation of the institutionalized sphere (in this case, the two dominating subsystems), men and women do not cease to be integrated by, and into, the 'life-world', specifically in a normative sense. Since I am presently discussing models, as opposed to concrete philosophical propositions, I will not follow any further Habermas's line of argumentation, but will instead replace it with my own. Systems integration is the integration of the specialized human, whereas social integration includes all newcomers to the world into the network of transsystemic communication in which they participate as whole humans. Social integration proceeds within the systems, but it is not accomplished by the systems. It is accomplished, as it has always been, by the sphere of objectivation in itself. In terms of this combination, one can come to the conclusion that each and every person (in modernity) is thrown into the *same* fundamental system, and his or her genetic *a priori* must therefore be dovetailed with this social *a priori*. Furthermore, the person is also dovetailed with the norms of transsystemic communication. The concrete normative requirement of each and every set of the sphere of 'objectivation in itself' may be entirely different, yet all of them will, or can, dovetail the genetic *a priori* with the social *a priori* of normative communication. A peson can thus shift as a whole from one locus to another without losing his or her abilities of normative understanding, which belong to those abilities that he or she acquired by the fundamental integration. This is a conflict model, for it is based on the conflict of two spheres of objectivation (that of 'in itself' and of 'for and in itself'), but it has a pessimistic cast. For here the fundamental sphere is obviously on the defensive, while the institutional sphere is on the offensive. A too vehement and successful offensive by the overwhelming sphere could easily disrupt the continuity of communicative integration of the life-world. The self-destruction of modernity can thus easily be conceived in terms of this model.

The third possible combination accompanies a completely different scenario (or view) of the institutional sphere. One can project a systemic world without one or two overwhelming systems that would devour the rest and would put an almost irresistible pressure on the life-world. One can further imagine that each institution (large or small) is a system in its own right, with all other systems as its environment, a view similar to Luhmann's. One particular system can be powerful enough to imprint other systems with its own logic. However, no system (institution) is powerful enough to influence all of them to the same degree. This scenario leaves us with a mosaic of subsystems of unequal power, weight and independence, but each with a certain amount of weight and relative independence. Assume that stratification happens according to functions that people perform in various institutions. If there is a 'mosaic' of institutions, the stratifiction patterns are perforce elastic, not rigid. One person can be placed high in one and low in another, and it is thus that social hierarchy becomes 'fluid'. Let us further assume the presence of 'social integration' of exactly the same kind as in the previous model or with some modifications of it. It is obvious that the world of institutions does not place an almost irresistible weight on the fundamental sphere, for the latter can also be offensive. Institutions can be opened up for normative criticism internally, and not just externally. Institutional patterns can be changed in certain institutions, which can in turn influence the learning processes of others, given that they are the environments of those others. Normatively based intervention is thus a far more concrete possibility. Last but not least, the person specialized in-and-for one or another institution, or type of institution, need not step out of the institution to regain their whole humanness. They can actually adopt the specialized attitude and the 'normal' attitude of the whole human person everywhere. If we compare this with the former model, we must arrive at the conclusion that, given that there are overwhelming systems (one or two), it is difficult to imagine how people as specialized persons can preserve their 'natural attitude', their normal, everyday normativity, or their communicative–normative competence, except for the fact that there are some institutions that have been institutionalized precisely for the conduct of such a discourse. However, from the standpoint of the person, this is just another function.

Let us assume that the sphere of objectivation in itself disappears or it becomes so emasculated that it cannot dovetail the genetic *a priori* with the social *a priori* of elementary norms and rules of human communication, interaction and 'doing things'. Even Huxley with his 'brave new world' could not begin to imagine such nightmarish fantasies. In Huxley, babies are immediately distributed among various institutionalized functions, and they are stratified by the institutionalized objectivation from the cradle. All loci and agencies of fundamental normative socialization (for example, the family) disappear. Yet even here, a minimal amount of transinstitutional communication must be preserved and mediated. This occurs via indoctrination, that is, institutionally. Obviously, without everyday socialization of a certain kind, without at least the preserved vestiges of the human person as a whole, the human condition would inevitably collapse. The model of complete institutionalization seems to be the model of chaos, for a total manipulative order *is* chaos. Chaos is not tantamount to a state of no rules. Rather, chaos is the state without norms and rules that would constitute the human condition, such norms and rules that can dovetail the social and the genetic *a priori* and introduce a new whole human person into the company of all other whole human persons.

Under what conditions then can the sphere of 'objectivation in itself' prevail and remain the main socializing factor in everyday life, in life pure and simple?

VIII

In my initial introduction of the concept of 'the human condition', I remarked that this sphere provides meanings in the plural, but not the singular. It is the sphere of 'objectivation for itself' that provides meaning (in the singular). This meaning is in turn filtered through the patterns of the fundamental sphere shaped by the patterns of the latter.

The sphere of 'objectivation in itself' ceased to be the major agency of social stratification in modernity. As we have seen, this development led to the contingency of the modern person. It also resulted in further transformations. The variations in the content of norms of this sphere result in a plurality without hierarchical organization. The person is thus free to leave one way of life and join another, or perhaps later several others. The density of the normative network also becomes a variable, and thus the tension resulting from the old kind of dovetailing of one *a priori* with the other is diminished by stepping out of a more dense normative network into a less dense one, or the other way round. Moreover, norms of everyday life are opened up for rational scrutiny, testing, re-confirmation and rejection, not only in terms of extreme tension, but continuously. We know that the normative universe as presented in the sphere of 'objectivation in itself' is taken for granted. As a result, one cannot query these norms by having recourse to the self-same objectivation. One has to have recourse either to the institutionalized sphere or to the sphere of objectivation for itself. In modern everyday life, men and women have direct access to the sphere of 'objectivation for itself'. They therefore do not need to subscribe to the meaning as it had been filtered through the primary objectivation. It was through this direct access to the sphere of 'objectivation for itself', as well as to a few universalized values that have occupied the status of 'quasi-objectivation for itself', that the process of the Enlightenment gathered momentum. At that stage, two danger zones made their appearance. It was believed that the constant de-legitimizing of everyday normative patterns would lead to a complete loss of meaning, to extreme relativism, doomsday and chaos. On the other hand, the demise of the sphere of 'objectivation for itself' appeared as a possibility on a nightmarish horizon. In the so-called 'nihilism narrative', lofty ideas themselves lead to the destruction of the elementary patterns of everyday life, while in the so-called manipulation discourse' the threat comes from a different quarter. It is presupposed that the entire sphere of 'objectivation for itself' becomes institutionalized and that it will be devoured by the institutionalized sphere. This is an additional side to the scenario of negative dialectics. The institutional sphere becomes omnipotent and it devours the subject after having successfully devoured the sphere of 'objectivation for itself'. The institutional sphere has the ability to learn, but it is incapable of creating meaning.

Does the person of everyday life have direct access to the sphere of 'objectivation for itself'? Can the person of everyday life raise himself or herself to the level of 'whole humanness', or do they practise what once was art, philosophy, religion and much else only as a 'specialized person', as a profession like all similar professions in the business of life? If the latter were the case, no other option would remain but one of empathy with, and support for, the anti-modernist drive, even if the latter is out to restore the hierarchical structure of the sphere of objectivation in itself, as well to bring us back to inequality and unfreedom, and drive us back into being a product of the 'dual accident'. And in fact, once the above positions are accepted as irresistible trends, the negative dialectic of modernity appears as an unstoppable logic. But there is no reason to subscribe to the above propositions. Rather, there is every reason to subscribe to those propositions that were delineated before them. All combinations are logically possible, but which of them has a real possibility remains to be seen. Yet something can be done to give momentum to one combination rather than to another.

IX

There are two basic models of social organization. As far as we can tell there is not a third, for social models are not invented by philosophers or sociologists; rather they can only be reconstructed, typified, modified on paper, within a theoretical paradigm. The first model we are familiar with provides stability together with systems of domination, power and hierarchy. The second model opens up possibilities which, for better or worse, can be developed. It is an unstable model. Contrary to the view that the closer humans remain to 'nature' (i.e. the simpler and more transparent human relations remain), the greater the threat or relapse into chaos, we have come to realize that the more overwhelming the institutionalized sphere becomes, the more developed the rule system is, the less stable our human condition becomes. In this state, the threat of chaos is in fact less remote than in other stages. The tension of our human condition has not diminished, it has only been dislocated or rather: relocated. It is now the tension among the three spheres. Each of these spheres must remain in place in order to preserve the fragile balance of our human condition.

The human condition in modernity resides in everyday life. Everyday life has to be guided by the primary sphere of objectivation. If this objectivation withers, the human condition vanishes along with it. Human beings cannot specialize without having first gained competence in everyday communication and interaction. In the modern version of human existence, such competence is gained by direct access to the sphere of 'objectivation for itself', to this sphere's non-institutionalized aspects.

Everyday life can be endangered and the human condition threatened, under the condition of modernity more than ever, owing to the fragile balance between the three spheres of objectivation, resulting from the cancerous growth of one of them. Still, there are three combinations of the spheres that could bring stability into the modern condition, and at least two of them can combine stability with greater openness, more equality and freedom than could have ever been posited in the finite versions of the first model. If one of these combinations will eventuate, we will be at the beginning of a new era, rather than at the end.

Notes

1   Georg Lukács, *Die Eigenart des Ästhetischen* (Neuwied/Rhein: Luchterhand, 1963).
2   Jürgen Habermas, *The Theory of Communicative Action* (Boston: Beacon Press, 1985, 1987).

3
Death of the Subject?

I

Before someone is buried, they need first to be identified. Otherwise, the alleged corpse may resume business right after the funeral. No autopsy has yet been performed on the thing or concept termed 'subject', though its demise is taken as a matter of fact by many students of philosophy. Actually, the concept 'subject' is polysemic to an extent that it lends itself easily to verbal and conceptual manoeuvring. An author can make a case against the subject in one of its interpretations, and then shift the argument in the direction of another, completely different, interpretation, without even noticing the shift. No wonder then that readers and interpreters are often guilty of being a party to mistaken identity.

In the contemporary French (and German) debates, the term 'subject' has assumed the following meanings: point of view; individual; the 'subject' of biography; the hermeneutic subject (meaning constituting subject); the subject who-gets-to-know (*Erkentnissubjekt*); the subject of knowledge (*Wissen*); the political subject (as both subjectum and subjectus); the moral subject (also as both subjectum and subjectus); person; personality; self; the mono-centred self; Ego; the man; self-consciousness; self-reflexivity; subject as Will; subject as Sovereignty; or simply the personal pronoun 'I'. In addition, the 'subject' includes all cases of non-individual, non-personal subjects, like the Kantian Transcendental Subject, the Hegelian World Spirit, or the Fichtean I, as well as personal, but non-human subjects, like God, and the so-called universal Subjects such as History, Humanism, Rights, Art and so on. Finally, if something is said about 'the subject' it is meant to be said also about 'subjective', 'subjectivity' and 'subjectivism'. The referents of the term 'subject' are slightly different in some cases, only remotely linked in some others, and sometimes have absolutely nothing in common or are entirely unrelated. The adjective 'subjective' and the nouns 'subjectivity' and 'subjectivism' are related to certain interpretations of the subject, whereas they are entirely unrelated to several others.

When someone talks about 'the subject', one has to ask first what kind of subject they are speaking about. Jean-Luc Nancy, for example (in *Le Partage des voix*), acclaims the 'end of the subject' given that real man has been sacrificed (in modernity) to Subjects such as Philosophy, Peace, Science, Art and History. Yet, when he writes that 'La voix de chacun est singulière' and that 'l'interpretation de l'universel est sa partition en voixs singulières' this sounds more like a declaration of love for the subject and as expression of hope in its re-birth rather than the gleeful announcement of the subject's well-deserved demise. Just ask yourself whether subject means to you primarily Philosophy, Art or Peace, or rather the singularity of your voice and that of the Other human creature; in all probability you will come down on the side of the second interpretation.[1]

The 'end of the subject' thesis is far from being new. Behaviourism preached it half a century ago; one of the greatest philosophical masterpieces of our century, Wittgenstein's *Philosophical Investigations*, can be interpreted as a statement on behalf of this thesis. The contemporary French wave, however, has very little to do with the Anglo-American tradition, in spite of Lyotard's numerous references to Wittgenstein's language-game theorem. In the Anglo-American tradition, the disappearance of the subject is an undramatic affair. Wittgenstein never made the existential dimensions of his philosophy explicit. In the strict behaviourist tradition, the subject is dismissed as a mythological device of pre-scientific thinking. It deserves mention that French structuralism – non-Marxist and Marxist alike – has also played the scientific versus unscientific card. The very assumption that there might be something like an individual 'subject', consciousness or will, was dismissed by structuralism as a fairytale for grown-up children. The structuralists, especially Althusser, convicted the 'philosophy of the subject' as guilty of humanism, i.e. unscientificity, a long time ago.[2]

The prehistory of the contemporary debate deserves a brief glance for obvious reasons. The political and philosophical development of many participants in the new wave took place under the influence of Althusserianism. The 'death of the subject' survived the demise of Marxism, and reappeared in a completely new guise. Now the concept of the 'subject' is rejected not because it is not scientific enough, but for the opposite reason; it is the 'subject' that created the havoc of science and technology. For one reason or another, it is always the subject that has to go.

In contrast to the drabness of behaviourism, the new wave of French ideology reintroduces the good old philosophical custom of presenting the thesis of the subject as a historical fiction. Quite a few philosophical narratives and meta-narratives are presently in the air. The speculative strength of these narratives is extremely divergent. I shall refer, very briefly, only to the two most dominant narrative clusters: the neo-Heideggerian and neo(post)-structuralist. Since each participant in the discourse presents his or her own version of the master narratives, I cannot do justice to any of them. I need to add that, even if narratives are fragmented, they remain fictions. Derrida is right that there are nothing but fragments.[3] I would only add that some create the illusion of having presented a whole; though in (post-)modern philosophy this rarely happens.

The Heideggerian fiction of the death of the subject unfolds on three levels. The first level is mystico-speculative, the second is meta-philosophical, the third meta-historico-political. Owing to the constant interplay of the three levels, a wide territory is opened up for theoretical speculation. One can speak all in one breath about the forgetfulness of Being, about the Subject of metaphysics and its vicissitudes, and about the doom that has been cast by metaphysics over the modern world in the form of technology (and democracy). The more weighty a philosophy is, the more divergent its interpretations – textual exegesis being, perhaps, the most subjective mode of interpretation. This is not meant as an insult, for 'subjective' can have both positive and negative connotations, at least in my mind, depending on the context. Interpretations (being sometimes textual exegeses of textual exegeses) can appear, among others, in the following composite fictions (I have purposely simplified the language of the fictions):

(1) The Subject as the brainchild of metaphysics disappears, whence metaphysics gets deconstructed; metaphysics is now going to be deconstructed, thus the subject disappears.

(2) The Subject was the brainchild of metaphysics, modern technology is the ultimate consumption of metaphysics where the forgetfulness of Being comes to pass (albeit technology is also the manifestation of Being). This scenario does not lend much support to the belief in the 'death of the subject', for we are now witnessing the exuberant presence of the 'actualization' of the Subject rather than its final demise.

(3) All this plus the deconstruction of the subject of philosophy (metaphysics) (and, maybe, also the presence of works of art) signal the coming end of the subject.

In all these combinations (and they are more complex and more sophisticated than by brief parody suggests) the 'death of the subject' is meant as something 'positive', if I am allowed to use a word from the metaphysical (and everyday) vocabulary. In the post-structuralist scenario, however, the same term refers to something 'dark, unwanted, or negative'. Foucault himself, who played an eminent part in the development of the second scenario, has preserved an aloofness, a playful pretence of mere descriptive objectivity. But this is not the emotional or intellectual experience of the reader who, reading Foucault, forms an opinion about prisons, mental asylums or the discourse of man or sexuality. Thus the negative evaluation of the 'end of the subject' is not a totally false and vulgar conclusion drawn by the uninitiated.

Now we say 'I speak' instead of 'I think'. The thinking person is 'something' inside, whereas the person who says, 'I speak', has nothing. In Foucault's formulation: 'Das Sein des Sprechens erscheint allein nur im Nichtdasein des Subjekts';[4] that is, the being of language appears in the non-being of the subject alone. This is why, so Foucault contends, the assertion 'I speak' plays the same role in modernity as 'I lie' did in ancient Greek thinking. There is no continuous development of a guilty metaphysics in Foucault. In his later books, he rather draws a strongly complimentary picture of ancient Greek (and even Roman) 'subjects', i.e. personalities. None the less, on many occasions, 'the subject' (and not only 'the man', an altogether different referent in Foucault's conceptual universe) resumes strongly negative connotations as being associated with 'mastering' and 'mastery', without any reference to the 'I speak' paradigm. The interpreter has also here a fairly broad hunting ground in his or her search for the demise of the subject.

I do not want to address the flaws of the master narratives. All philosophical fictions are flawed if read as real stories and not as allegories or metaphors as they should be. It is easy to point out that it took two thousand years for metaphysics to arrive at its destination, modern technology, and thus the 'connection' between the two events is so fantastic that the development of the Hegelian World Spirit looks like sober realism when compared with the Heideggerian myth of metaphysics. It is even easier to point out that we can devise alternative fictions. The question that remains open is the speculative yield that such alternative narratives may bring. Mere refutations of the empirical trustworthiness of master narratives normally bear fairly poor speculative yield. Original counter-fictions may bring more attractive results. There is no doubt in my mind that after the 'death of the subject' narratives are, at least temporarily, exhausted, the counter-fictions will share their fate.

No philosophical statement can relativize itself. Most of the 'end of the subject' narratives are simultaneously 'end of philosophy' fictions as well, given that Philosophy (or metaphysics) is said to be guilty of producing the Subject or of being the Subject incarnate. No one could ever imagine a scientific statement declaring the end of science or a religious statement proclaiming the end of religion. The emphasis on the 'end of philosophy', however, fits smoothly into the tradition of philosophy; it is the philosophical tradition *par excellence*. Since philosophers believe that there is only one philosophy (theirs), they must claim the end of philosophy in the same breath, and so they do. The difference is that moderns, or at least some of the post-moderns, defer the claim to truth instead of suggesting the tasteless alternative that there is no truth. Yet, whatever they do, they remain within the confines of philosophical language games. It is very easy to prove this point. The best among them bring forth a world (a philosophical edifice) and furnish it with categories, tricks and rules of the game. They invite others for a visit or a stay. Whoever enters that world will be at home there. He or she will constantly rearrange the (existing) furniture, play the pre-given tricks and play them according to the rules; he or she will interpret and modify the categories to the extent that the world of that philosophy permits. Those who enter the world of a philosophy accept the world's language as their natural tongue, they speak it, and they think in accordance with it. They will be outraged if a person who has not stepped into the same world declares that they are just talking nonsense, that the things they refer to 'do not exist', and they will be right. But those others will be right too, for the zealots of a streamlined philosophical edifice exclude them from the world of speculation: either you subscribe to the end of philosophy and of the subject, or you are not philosophers at all. True enough, one can interpret Heidegger as the opponent of the perpetual war in philosophy, and point out with him that works of art do not fight against one another. Certainly, works of art do not fight, even if artists do; however philosophies themselves fight, and not just philosophers. The young Lukács once suggested that works of art are closed worlds, cold stars that bring warmth only to the recipients, and I have added that they are the mirror images of our existential solitude. Philosophies, on the other hand, are mirror images of our unsocial sociability. The talk about the 'end of philosophy' ends only with philosophy. As long as the fiction of 'end of' something, or – alternatively – the birth of something, continues, philosophy is alive and kicking.

Precisely because philosophy is the mirror image of our unsocial sociability, we do not choose a philosophy at random. In taking up a philosophical position, we take up a position in the network of unsociable sociability, of conflicts, alliances, abuses, loves, friendships, that is, a network of affections and commitments. And precisely because philosophy is just the mirror image of our unsocial sociability, we can allow our philosophical taste to have the lion's share in the choice. One does not subscribe to a too pedestrian philosophy with enthusiasm even if it fits well with one's commitment. And one cannot help admiring speculative strengths and letting oneself be carried away by them up to the point where serious commitment loudly protests.

Some contemporary authors, among them Habermas, whom I deeply respect, identify philosophy too much with the network of unsociable sociability, and tend to forget that it is just a mirror image, a metaphor, a game. At the other extreme, some tend to forget that philosophy is not void of moral and political commitment, precisely because it is the mirror image of our unsociable sociability. When someone carries their Heideggerianism to the extreme that makes humanism the main culprit for Nazism,[5] they definitely cross the dividing line between a serious game and an irresponsible one. To assert that one of the interpretations of the subject, namely that of absolute creativity (autoproduction), can also result in totalitarianism is one thing, but to conflate autoproduction with humanism *in toto* is another. If philosophers tamper with the interpretation of momentous political events, they need to scrutinize their categories more thoroughly than they otherwise might. Autocreativity is, and has been, one – and not even the major – interpretation of humanism throughout history, our modern history included. If they do not elaborate the alternative interpretations of the concept that have all been on a collision course with Nazism, philosophers sacrifice things that they, as people, stand for, in order to score a good point in a philosophical game.

In our world of unsociable sociability all positions can be occupied. Many positions can also be populated by a considerable variety of philosophies, all of which will try to exclude some, while allying themselves with certain others.

Given that the slogan about the 'end of the subject' is most associated (with or without justification) with the other slogan 'anything goes', I must comment briefly upon the latter.

'Anything goes' can mean the following: the language game called philosophy permits a great variety of novel combinations and, in principle, no gambit is excluded from the genre. Spectators (of philosophy) adopt this standpoint fairly easily. Philosophical actors could also subscribe to this version of relativism without endangering the survival of this unique species of imagination. I, for my part, declare myself ready for this brand of relativism – would that a few philosophers would join me by manifesting similar readiness. Statements such as: 'one cannot philosophize this way anymore', 'the paradigm of language is the only paradigm of philosophy' 'the paradigm of consciousness is totally outdated', and so on and so forth, swamp philosophical discourse. If Nietzsche was the last metaphysician, then metaphysics is gone forever, and if someone still practises metaphysics they certainly manifest only a lack of philosophical sensitivity. Philosophy is still perceived, and not just by some preachers of the end of the subject, as a kind of technological device, like a computer that becomes outdated after the introduction of a new model.

'Anything goes' can mean also the following: one philosophy is as good or as bad as any other; none of them is more true than any other. No philosophical actor can possibly take up this position, and none ever did. One cannot stake one's personality or unleash one's imagination to bring forth a world where one and others can dwell, and assert from the selfsame standpoint that 'anything goes'. One can certainly switch from the standpoint of the actor to that of a spectator, and then assert that 'anything goes'. The spectator can be a perfect hermeneutician, a hermeneutician through and through. But philosophers are never perfect hermeneuticians while dwelling in the house of their own philosophy. Whether they constitute a Subject or not, whether they construct or de-construct, is of very little relevance here.

Whenever someone offers you a world in which you can dwell, a language that you can speak esoterically, a framework of speculation where you can toy with many dominant and subdominant elements, you must know that this world (or language game) was not thought out by the perfect hermeneutician, nor will you be one as long as you find satisfaction in toying with the dominant or subdominant elements of this world. This world is an individual, for you can identify it in all its difference (many books and studies). It is a meaning-carrying individual, which interprets (self-interprets) and lends itself to practically infinite interpretations, but not to all kinds of interpretation. It is a self (of course, not a mono-centred one) by virtue of its dominant and subdominant elements. And, if it is modern, it is also a subject, for it bears the hallmark of contingency, which has been pulled together into a personal destiny. The subject in the text and the subject of the text together can be termed 'dogmatism' or the 'fix point' or the 'centre' or the cachet or the birthmark, call it what you will. This is the subject I am going to talk about. More precisely, I am going to speak not about the subject of the philosopher as an actor (author), but about the subject of men and women (what makes modern actorship and authorship first possible).

As already indicated, concepts like subject, subjective, subjectivity and subjectivism need to be distinguished. For brevity's sake let me corroborate this by a few references to the history of modern philosophy. The term 'subjective' normally indicates inferiority in contrast with the 'objective' in both Kant and Hegel, the two main defendants in the trial against the Subject in the contemporary debate. In contrast, it was Kierkegaard who challenged all Hegelians by claiming that truth is subjective, and he was certainly not a champion of logocentrism. Subjectivity, on the other hand, is frequently identified with inwardness, also in Hegel. Subjectivism has been attributed to the cultivation of the subjective point of view together with the claim of individuality for unrestricted self-realization, and is generally associated with the romantic school. Subjectivism was strongly disapproved of by both Hegel and Kierkgaard, for the latter's enthusiastic plea for subjectivity was not an endorsement of subjectivism. I have restricted my brief references to our tradition to the understanding of individual subjects prior to (or irrespective of) the differentiation between epistemological, moral and political subjects. My own comments will follow next.

II

Whatever is termed 'subject' in contemporary philosophy, it is certainly thought of not as an empirical human universal, but as a real or imaginary entity, feature, attitude, propensity, which happens to belong to occidental history, or just to the modern world. I accept this view as a starting point. Occidental or European history is a modern text that incorporates certain pre-modern traces or testimonies and juxtaposes others as its opposite, its 'alter'. Since we share modern history, we cannot escape being party to the exegesis of the modern text. One can make an attempt at historical transcensus, to challenge the limits of our horizon. In fact, Heidegger attempts just this. I am not joining him, but prefer to clarify our own historical consciousness within the limits of our historical horizon.

There is a novel (and a film) with the title *The World According to Garp*. Neither the novel nor the film interests us here, only the title. There is a person called Garp, so there is also a world according to Garp. If there is a person called Joh Piper, there is also a world accoridng to Joh Piper. There is a world according to every person who dwells here, in modernity. This is what I am going to call *subject*.

The first autobiography was written by Augustine. It was not about the world according to Augustine, but about the representative ascent to Truth. The first 'European' autobiographies were written in the period of the Renaissance. But Cardano did not describe the world according to Cardano, nor Cellini the world according to Cellini – they committed to paper the unusual, unique adventures that were experienced by the man Cardano or by the man Cellini in the world. Rousseau's *Confessions* can be rendered as 'the world according to Rousseau' by us. Yet Rousseau himself would have protested against such an enormous impertinence. His confessions were not the confessions of a contingent person, but the confessions of a represent-ative personality; and the world, too, was meant to be representative, not just a world according to Jean-Jacques.

Let us cast a random glance over recent publications. The book market is swamped with life stories, success stories, failure stories and all else. Schlegel once said that everyone can write at least one good novel, his or her autobiography. I would date the emergence of the subject from this statement rather than from the Cartesian *cogito*. That everyone can write a (good) novel about themselves is questionable if good is understood as high artistic quality. Yet, if it is understood as engaging, or even interesting, reading, Schlegel proved to be a great prophet. If someone was only a little bit known as an actor or an actress, a singer, a director, a criminal, a businessman, a painter, a writer, a boxer, a baseball player, the son or the daughter, the sister or brother of the above, a politician of any renown, or even his secretary or factotum, one expects them to write their autobiography. All of them can expect to be widely read. If they cannot write, their autobiography will be taped and written down by someone else. Can we attribute this thirst for autobiography to mere curiosity, to our irresistible desire for eavesdropping or peeping through the keyhole? The taste for gossip is old, but the general drive to write autobiographies (and biographies) is new. Moreover, autobiographies are read even if one is completely ignorant in the field of the author's celebrity, or if the author is no celebrity at all, just that they happened to write about their life.

In modern autobiographies there is a dual authorship. The person is the *author of the text* (whether written or taped) and he or she is the *author of his or her own life*. To put it more cautiously, he or she is supposed to be the author of his or her own life, as he or she is supposed to be the author of his or her text. The dual authorship guarantees the truth content. The authors are expected to present the reader with a true world, in a dual understanding once again. They are expected to be truthful, that is, to relate a 'real' story (one is not supposed to write fiction as autobiography); and they are also expected to present a world (or rather two worlds, one internal and one external) as they see it, experience it and assess it; this is a world 'according to them'. Even the most pedestrian autobiography full of chunks of stereotyped banalities needs the makebelieve of a world that is the author's own making. To endorse Schlegel, men and women normally succeed beyond all expectations in presenting a world 'according to them'. They happen to present themselves as subjects.

Can we say that the world according to Joh is the subject of Joh? Or can we say that Joh *is* a subject who presents himself in a specific, subject-related interpretation of the world? Or can we say that Joh *as* a subject does the same?

That there is a world according to (Joh) is the subject (of Joh); yet the world according to Joh is not the subject of Joh. The world is not a subject at all, for there is no world according to the world, or, at least, this proposition does not make sense in the framework of my present speculations. In order for there to be a world according to Joh there must be a world first. Everything said about the human condition in

Chapter 2 naturally applies to Joh. Joh, like all other human beings, was born into a meaningful human universe. He, like everybody, was also born with the destiny to be related to all other bodies by meaning. He has received the network of meanings from his social universe. They were embedded in, and mediated by, the norms and rules of ordinary language, of the use of objects, and in the customs of his environment. Joh, like all other Johs before him, started his life in making out the meanings of the received meanings, while filling out the received meaning with his personal experience. Objects were given to his inborn drives (like proper food to his hunger), yet he developed a taste of his own. He was taught how and when to manifest his innate affects (like fear), yet he became courageous or a coward. Tasks were given to him (e.g. to cultivate a plot of land) and he did better or worse; his best innate propensities became developed or remained barren. Every Joh became thus a single person different from all others. Before learning the importance of sentences like 'I think' or 'I speak', he certainly learned the importance of the utterance 'I feel'. Every Joh is the navel of his universe.

Had our occidental Joh been born a few hundred years ago (or probably less) he would have received not only the network of meanings but also the general explanation of all of them. He would have learned why everything is as it is and why it should be so; why the stars shine, why people die, and what happens to them after they have died. So he would have received a fairly complete map of the external and internal world. Had our occidental Joh been born a few hundred years ago, there would not have been a world 'according to Joh', for there was no subject.

Let us proceed to the second question. Is Joh himself the subject we talk about? Is there a world 'according to Joh' because Joh (the subject) manifests itself in this world?

Subject can mean 'being subjected to' or 'subjecting something to'. In the modern philosophical vocabulary 'subject' is normally juxtaposed with 'object'. I could even add an unorthodox variation to the theme by rendering the meaning of subject as 'being related to something or someone'. Yet, orthodox or unorthodox, no interpretation of the 'subject' can possibly identify it with Joh or with anyone else.

Joh is, indeed, 'subjected to' several things. *What* he is subjected to is a historical variable (such as God, the sovereign, the constitution, the law of nature, the moral law), and, at least sometimes, open to interpretation and choice. But, whatever Joh is subjected to, he is never identical with his being-subjected-to. If Joh is a slave, he is not identical with himself-as-a-slave – if for no other reason, simply because he also subjects something to himself and is related to something else. Hegel, in the celebrated chapter on Master and Slave in his *Phenomenology of Spirit*,[6] presented the model of this dialectical turn and twist.

Many things are, indeed, subjected to Joh, and so are persons. *What* he subjects to his will is a historical variable, and sometimes open to interpretation and choice. (A Joh subjects the land while tilling it, yet another Joh shares the belief of having subjected nature as such; one Joh subjects his wives and children to his will, yet another Joh in other times will, perhaps, decide not to.) But whatever Joh subjects to his will, he is never identical with the practice of subjecting-to, if for no other reason, simply because he is also subjected to something, and because he also relates to something else.

The same could be said about Joh's 'being related to something'.

Joh as subjecting something, as being subjected to something and as being related to something *taken together* are still *not* Joh. Joh thinks, talks and feels many things in conjunction with these three relations. If two Johs subjected the same things to their will and were also subjected to the same persons and things, they would still remain different persons, and not only in their external appearances. Yet it is not this triviality I wanted to arrive at.

If Joh is not a subject, what *is* he then?

We can answer this question easily: Joh is a human person. This is a correct answer, but an irrelevant one in our quest for the subject. Since we began this quest with the intention of pinning down the subject in 'the world according to Joh', the abstract identity of a person with all the other persons cannot play a role in our enquiry, not even as the exemplification of what the subject is not. Only a theory of a collective Subject (with a capital S) needs to talk about human persons stripped of all their personal and cultural identification marks. And yet the sentence 'Joh is a subject' and the other sentence 'Joh is a human person' are closely linked. More precisely, they are linked *historically*. To this question I will shortly return.

The question still needs to be answered: if Joh is not a subject, what *is* he then?

Space does not allow us to identify our Joh as a Frenchman, as a merchant, and so on, and to show that all such and similar identifications are ultimately irrelevant for our enquiry.

We left our Joh (who had been thrown into a world by the accident of being born just then and there) as he started to cope with this accident, and became such-and-such a single person, different from all other single persons. He *is* a single person, he *is* this-and-this particular unique person. This is what he actually is. But he can be (become) a this-and-this unique person in two different ways. Becoming a unique person in one way or in another does not merely make a difference, it makes *the* difference. For the unique person can remain unique as a particular single being or can become an individual or a personality. Joh is either a particular single being or a unique personality (obviously he can also be some kind of a mixture of both).

Joh is a particular single being and remains one in the process of dual identification. He identifies himself entirely with the world he takes for granted, as he also identifies himself entirely with himself. Put bluntly, he identifies himself with the two *a priori* of his very existence: the genetic *a priori* and the social *a priori*. All his experiences are organized around the two *a priori*: since they are accidental, but he is unaware of their accidental character, he himself becomes entirely accidental. In contrast, the individual unique person (personality) never identifies himself or herself with the world as it is, neither does he or she identify himself or herself entirely with himself or herself. A personality reflects upon the world and upon himself or herself. His or her experiences are synthetic in character for he or she ceases to be accidental and becomes his or her own destiny.

It would be the greatest blunder to identify the individual personality with the subject in any of the latter's current interpretations. Certainly, the historical conditions of modernity, especially of early modernity, favoured the self-development of personalities of this kind. It is also true that the *modus operandi* of modernity does not put as severe a constraint upon personality development as most pre-modern societies did. But all this does not mean that 'the subject' and the individual personality are identical. The referents are different (for Joh *is* a personality, but he *is not* a subject) and there is, in addition, no necessary connection between the two. There were many outstanding individuals in ancient societies, yet one could hardly talk about Oedipus or Moses as 'subjects'. In fact, Hegel and many other thinkers of his time predicted the demise of personalities in the modern world (the time of the subject) and not without foundation. If you wish, you can also associate the birth of the subject with the birth of pettiness. If you agree that Joh's subject is the world according to Joh, then subject can be tied both to a person of unreflected singularity and to a person of individual personality. The lack of reflexivity and complete self-identification as well as total identification with the environment (that is, narcissism and conformity) do not prevent any Joh from conjuring up a world 'according to Joh'; experience teaches rather the opposite.

Having found out what Joh is, and what he can become, it suffices to repeat that he is not a subject. Yet even if this were true, could we still suggest that a person (this time we call her Jill) manifests herself or expresses herself *as* a subject in the world 'according to Jill'?

Mentioning Jill *as* a subject is to presume that Jill *has* certain features, faculties or capacities that can be termed her subject. Spatial thinking normally places this 'subject' of Jill inside the body of Jill.

That our conscious and unconscious 'inside' is not homogeneous is so obvious that one would be unlikely to find primitive cultures that knew it otherwise. Mythologies and other fictions explain this most fascinating and most commonly perceived wonder and many a map of the soul has been drawn and provided by religions and philosophies alike. That our so-called interior is not homogeneous is such an obvious experience that we can compare it only to the experience of seeing or hearing. We actually do not even need to become acquainted with (*erkennen*) this phenomenon given that we know it (*kennen*). What we need to receive, and what we actually do receive from the representative fictions, is *meaning*. Since we are bodies who are connected to all other bodies by meaning, we are surely connected to our own body by meaning. It is from the standpoint of the above (provided) meanings that we understand or interpret our own 'inside'; thus we make sense of our pre-cognitive intuitions.

Jill, our next door neighbour, is in a predicament. Unlike her great-grandmother who understood herself as being composed of a mortal body and an immortal soul, she has no firm solace. Jill is approached and bombarded by at least a dozen entirely different and competing interpretations of her 'interior', and, alas, all of them do make sense of one kind or another, so she cannot figure out for sure what kind of map she is carrying inside. Could we, perhaps, maintain that doing something *as* a subject, or manifesting oneself *as* a subject, amounts to the following two-step procedure: first, one interprets one's own interior by a meaningful world-view and draws the map of one's interior by using an original draft-map of the world-view in question; and, second, one manifests this 'map' in understanding the world. The world according to Jill would then be a world that succeeds in manifesting the map Jill is carrying inside, as interpreted and perceived by Jill herself.

Just as Jill's predicament is modern, so is the subject. There is certainly a connection between Jill's predicament and the emergence of the subject. If there is not one single meaningful world-view or a conglomeration of a few world-views that provide the model-map for understanding the inside of us all, but rather just a marketplace where any world-view is freely exchangeable for any other, then there are no model-maps available for making out the meaning of the world, or anything in the world. There is, indeed, a congruency between the contingency of the internal map and the external map, yet there is no reason to believe that the external map will somehow express or manifest the internal map. The 'world according to Jill', that is, the subject of Jill, can hardly be identified with the direct manifestation of the internal map Jill is carrying inside her body, at least in her own perception.

The map of the interior can be termed the *self*. Since our spiritual interior was practically never perceived as homogeneous, there was never a mono-centred self – understood in terms of the fixed centrepoint of a circle. But in a completely different interpretation, the term 'mono-centred self' makes perfect sense. The map is then hierarchically ordered, where the centre is its most powerful agent. This can be a peak called Reason, towering above the plains, or a tremendous waterfall, termed Passion, sweeping away everything that gets in its way. The gist of the matter is, however, that the centre of the map termed the self (if there is such a centre) is never the centre of the self. For the centre of the self (if there is such a centre) is *outside* the self, it is 'in' the world. The centre of the self is neither Reason nor Passion; everything can be that centre if referred to by a possessive pronoun. The centre of Jill's self (she is not mono-centred) is her beloved, her child, her political commitment, her profession. Everything that is mine can be one of the centres of my self (passion or reason, too, among others), though not everything that is mine is in the centre of my self, or even on the periphery of my self. Only a few issues, people, things, goals, propensities that are mine can be the centres of my self; they become really mine exactly because they are one of the centres of my self. The 'world according to Jill' will encapsulate these centres of Jill's self.

We know that Jill has not inherited a master map of the soul to guide her self-understanding; neither did she receive from her ancestors a master narrative to guide her understanding of the world. Now we come to know about her third privation, namely that she has not inherited any ideal or real object as the centre of her self and, in this sense, as *hers* by birthright. These three privations together amount to a bunch of open possibilities. The bunch of open (because indeterminate) possibilities equals contingency. Modern men and women are contingent; they are also aware of their contingency. Mere possibilities are empty, yet they can be filled with an infinite variety of contents. Mere possibility is the potential of personal autonomy; it is also the potential of a total loss thereof. Modern men and women are unstable and fragile, yet they seek some solidity; they easily stumble into chaos, so they need at least a fragment of 'cosmos' to make sense of their own lives and, possibly, render meaning to it.

Jill *is* Jill – a unique, particular person. A modern Jill – such as many other Jills before her – can develop two, distinct attitudes to the world (her own, interior, world included): the attitude of unreflected singularity and the attitude of individual personality.

Since Jill does not receive her destiny's broad outlines in her cradle, she has to destine herself to become an individual personality. To destine oneself is to choose oneself. As we know, the centre of the self is not an item on the map of the soul, it is just the thing, the person, the cause we are involved in, beyond and above everything else. Choosing oneself thus means to choose the focuses around which our personality begins to develop. In choosing oneself (the centres of our self) we become what we are: this or that kind of individual personality.

Kierkegaard once said that if you do not choose yourself you let others choose for you. If Jill fails to choose herself, she lets others choose for her. This was not an alternative for Jill's great-grandmother, who received her destiny, at least in broad outline, in her cradle. Great-grandmother Jill could have developed a reflective relation to herself and the tradition, or she could have followed the tradition and those persons who embodied it (her father, husband and priest). These others, and, by extension, tradition, would have decided for her. Our modern Jill is born as a bundle of empty possibilities. When she fails to choose herself, she lets other contingent persons choose for her. The end result, the narcissistic conformist, is well known.

Let me return for the last time to the problem of the centres of the self. I referred to those centres by the term 'objects'. 'Object' stands here for a *being*-in-the-world and objects for 'beings'-in-the-world, where 'being' is not capitalized. Objects-in-the-world are related to subjects. Yet the centre of the self is the centre of the *self* and not of the 'subject'. The subject of Jill is (in our definition) the world according to Jill – not Jill as a person, not Jill's self, not Jill's personality (if she has one), not her unreflected singularity (if she failed to choose herself). The object is what appears in the centre(s) of the self as being presented in the world according to Jill (her subject). The world according to Jill is the subject of Jill, and what appears at the centre is the object(s). This object(s) could possibly be chosen by Jill, but Jill could also have failed to choose, and, if she did, the objects of Jill would be chosen by others, not by Jill. But whether the first or the second is the case, there will certainly be a world according to Jill (a subject) and a centrepoint (or a few centrepoints) of this world (objects). The subject–object relation is not an epistemological relation, but a historico-ontological one.

Subject is the idiosyncracy of the interpretation of human world experience and self-experience under the condition of modernity.

Modern men and women manifest their being-in-the-world idiosyncratically. Whether they are (become) unreflected singularities or individual personalities, they all manifest their being-in-the-world as subjects. The world according to a conformist narcissist is a subject no less than the world of a personality. However, the equally idiosyncratic worlds are still different in kind. One Jill chooses herself and thereby also her main involvements (objects). The world according to her will centre around the issues of her involvements. So she gets as close as one ever can to what was once called subject/object identity. The other Jill, who lets others choose for her, will manifest the 'objects' of her self, these fragments of alien meanings, as firm and uncontestable truths whenever they support her narcissism, and as blatant untruths whenever they affront her network of self-identifications. What is idiosyncratic here (the world according to our second Jill) is the ever-changing character of the pendulum movement between unreflected other-identification and unreflected self-identification.

There are many narratives of the 'end of the subject' and all of them are entirely idiosyncratic in the form they happened to be first told by their authors. Sometimes our epoch is compared to Hellenism, with very little justification. Stoicism, Epicureanism, Scepticism and Platonism were professed and practised by thinkers for more than a millenium and beyond. It was the common world that reigned supreme, in philosophy maybe even more than in social and political life. But on our tree of philosophy no two leaves are alike; some leaves do not even resemble others. One sometimes gets the impression that the fury of innovation has completely enchanted what is now termed philosophy; evil tongues talk about fashion, competition and market by way of explanation.

In fact, many a modern philosophy is recycled, though in remarkably idiosyncratic ways. These recycled versions of the old participate in the world of idiosyncratic quasi-monads. Philosophical mini-narratives are quasi-monads only because the sole quality that makes them monads is their idiosyncracy, their difference. Mini-narratives are not closed but open; they collide with one another, they go in to combat, they are even sensitive to social change. This is how philosophy remains the mirror image of our unsocial sociability. Yet the monads are also influence-resistant; their receptivity threshold is extremely high and as a result very little real discourse goes on among them (philosophies of discourse are no exception).

The narratives of the end of the subject are extremely strong statements about both personalities and subjects. In fact, the narratives encapsulate worlds according to those contemporary philosophers. They are subjects; moreover they are *representative subjects*. The less we want them to be representative subjects, the more they become one. Not even philosophers can jump over their own shadows.

Notes

1 Jean-Luc Nancy, *Le Partage des voix* (Paris: Editions Galilee, 1982). The 'end of the subject' is also proclaimed in a similar vein in F. Lacoue-Labarthe, *La Fiction du politique* (Strasbourg; University of Strasbourg, 1987); J. Derrida, *D l'Esprit, Heidegger et la question* (Paris: Editions Galilee, 1987). For a polemical treatment, see Luc Ferry and A. Renaut, *Heidegger et les Modernes* (Paris: Grasset, 1988).

2 Althusserianism was embraced primarily for this reason. Althusser played out the 'mature' Marx, who had allegedly left humanism and the subject far behind, to the young (not-yet-mature) author of still partly 'humanistic' works.

3 Discussed in J. Derrida, *Spurs: Nietzsche's styles* (Chicago: University of Chicago Press, 1979).

4 M. Foucault, *La Pensée du dehors*. Quoted from *Schriften zur Literatur* (Frankfurt: Ullstein, 1979), p. 133.

5 This opinion is strongly represented by Lacoue-Labarthe.

6 G. W. F. Hegel, *Phenomenology of the Spirit* (*Mind*), Section B, Chapter IV, Sub-section a.

4
Are We Living in a World of Emotional Impoverishment?

I

Women and men normally associate emotions with feelings.[1] 'Being in an emotional state' (that is, being angry, being full of joyous expectations, being anxious, etc.) is tantamount to *feeling* something. Behaviourism, as well as certain branches of cognitive psychology, do not accept this everyday experience at its face value. It insists that emotions are in fact cognitive–evaluative processes and, for that reason, they cannot be understood as 'feelings'. However, one can accept the premise without subscribing to the conclusion. From Plato's *Philebus* to Aristotle's *Rhetoric*, philosophy established the venerable tradition of understanding emotions as cognitive and situated feelings. On the one hand, this means that emotions affect judgement. On the other, it means – and this is the pre-eminent issue here – that the kind and intensity of a particular emotion are dependent upon our understanding of a situation. 'The frame of mind is that in which any pain is being felt', Aristotle remarks,[2] and this is true also of all kinds of pleasure. The juxtaposition of reason and emotion is a heuristic device forged by rationalist philosophies. If something went wrong with this device, it will not be rectified by transferring emotions into the bracket of 'the cognitive' while leaving feelings and the body stranded on the wrong side of the great dividing line.

Let us then accept, as a starting point, that emotions, as well as sentiments, are feelings. Let us further accept that emotions, to the same extent as sentiments, are also cognitive and judgemental processes. Granted this, the link between the feeling aspect and the judgemental aspect of a particular emotion can still be theorized in a different manner. One can assume that there are two (or more) 'unspecific' feelings, like the feeling of pain and the feeling of pleasure, which occur *in conjunction with* our evaluation of situations or persons. The feeling aspect is always unchanged, for it is the evaluation that defines them, that makes them perceived as a particular emotion. For example, the same feeling of displeasure (discomfort) is defined/perceived on one occasion as grief, another time as envy, and yet another time as anxiety or as expectation of bad news, and the like. Certain experiences lend credence to this view. For example, sometimes we feel displeasure without being able to give the feeling a name, simply because we are not aware of its causes. Yet once we find 'reasons for feeling displeasure', if at all, we can identify the feeling as, for example, 'expectation of bad news', 'pangs of conscience', 'being angry', and so on. In other words, we identify it as a distinct emotion.

However, sometimes we are unable to identify the feeling irrespective of the emotional terms applied to their description. Moreover, in such situations we often feel, and this too is a feeling, that no emotional term can describe (express) properly the quality of our feelings. We then try to circumscribe our particular unique feeling via the combination of several emotional terms. This second and elementary experience suggests that our feelings are rather unique and qualitatively distinct. Furthermore it suggests that the relationship of our emotions to their cognitive component is not merely external: the cognitive–evaluative–situational aspect is inherent in the very feeling itself. The fact that the emotional terms do not really do justice to the complexity of our feelings lends further support to the thesis of inherence. The emotional term 'to be afraid' is an umbrella term for several qualitatively different feelings. An obvious objection to this would be that the cognitive aspect resides not just in the emotional term but also in the concrete situation (as well as in the evaluation of this situation) in which the emotional term is used (for example, 'being afraid of being found out', 'being afraid of death', 'being afraid of an examination', and so on).

In my view, both kinds of experience tell us something about emotions. If the cognitive–evaluative aspect of emotions inheres in the feeling itself, we then have a variety of shades of feelings that are qualitatively distinct and we will also have the (secondary) feeling that prefabricated emotional terms and expressions do not do justice to these distinct shades of feeling. If the connection between the feeling and the cognitive–evaluative–situational aspect of the emotion remains merely external, we will have no problem in identifying our pleasure or displeasure (comfort–discomfort, pleasure–pain, to list the distinctions in terms of their intensity) with the emotional expression adequate to them. Furthermore, certain situations or persons will invariably elicit the same particular feelings in us – for example: 'beauty therefore appeal', 'competition therefore envy', 'enemy of my community therefore hatred'.

Something similar can be asserted about sentiments. Sentiments are emotional dispositions. 'Having a sentiment' or 'being in a sentiment' (such as friendship or love of any kind) does not indicate the constant and continuous presence of one and the same feeling or emotion. It rather indicates the presence of a disposition to develop certain feelings and emotions every time the object of our sentiment, or our relation to the object of our sentiment, is affected. Whenever the cognitive–evaluative aspect of the emotion inheres in the sentiment itself, one's love or friendship felt for different people, ideas or things will be qualitatively distinct. In such a situation, one's world of feeling will be like a palette with all shades of colours on it. Contrariwise, whenever the cognitive–evaluative aspect of the sentiment is externally related to the simple feelings of pleasure–displeasure (and all their versions in terms of intensity), the same 'condition' will always evoke the same emotional response and one will never face the problem of identifying one's sentiments.

II

Emotions as well as sentiments can be good or bad, strong or weak, deep or superficial. However, it is not so easy to translate the whole emotional universe of a person into such categories. One can say tentatively that a person's emotions and sentiments are weak even if a few of their emotions make themselves felt 'strongly'. Similarly, a man can be described as 'emotionally deep' despite our awareness of several rather superficial sentiments in him. If the moral yardstick ('good or bad') serves as the criterion of categorization, neither frequency (of occurrence) nor numerical superiority (of one feeling over the others) will be decisive. A single evil passion can render a person's whole emotional universe evil in our final judgement.

However, irrespective of the difficulties in the evaluation of a particular case, the criteria of evaluation are eminently clear. Traditional character types (melancholic, choleric, and so on) were constructed on the basis of everyday observation; they undoubtedly centre on combinations of deep–superficial and strong–weak emotional 'units'. The moral assessment is different in kind. Therefore it does not yield clusters of temperamental character, although both 'good' and 'bad' can show a strong affinity with intensity. The 'proper' feeling response should not be too weak nor should it be too strong. Aristotle's theory of the proper mean explores exactly this situation.

The binary category 'rich–poor' has, at first glance, a distinctive feature in contrast with all others: one cannot be characterized as either rich or poor on the basis of single emotions. An instance of fear or anger can be strong or weak, deep or superficial, good or bad, but it cannot be either rich or poor. However, a sentiment can be rich or poor because, as an emotional disposition, it may give rise to quite different kinds and shades of a great variety of emotions, as well as to other feelings which cannot be discussed within this framework. In a similar fashion, the emotional universe of a person can be termed rich and poor respectively. Yet it is not accidental that the distinction between a 'rich' and a 'poor' emotional world cannot be translated back into the old categories of human temperaments. Emotional poverty or wealth obviously has nothing to do with temperament or, for that matter, with the emotional terms of the denizens of that ancient world whose image shaped the clusters of the types of temperament.

On second thoughts, one can even wonder whether the designation of a person's whole emotional universe in terms of poor and rich can be taken for granted. We are used to these appellations and we completely understand how to appraise the poverty or wealth of a person's emotional universe. But was the inner world of Odysseus's or Don Quixote's emotions rich or poor? Without quite artificial intellectual efforts and devices, these questions cannot be properly answered, for the question itself seems somehow to be misplaced. Whereas the same question would be properly posed if asked about the heroes and heroines of eighteenth–nineteenth-century novels. Titles like *Sense and Sensibility* needed no further interpretation in those centuries.

Hegel praised the ancient world for its plasticity. The modern world however lacks plasticity. Modern, 'romantic' art excels in painting, poetry and music; they are the genres *par excellence* of subjectivity. The enquiry into the character of the subject (undertaken in Chapter 3) did not elaborate the problem of subjectivity. The subject was described as the idiosyncracy of the interpretation of human world experience and self-experience under the condition of modernity. Subjectivity can be understood as the self-reflexivity of the subject.

The emotional life of men and women can be rich or poor under the condition of 'subjectivity' thus understood alone. The fact that the subjects themselves are intersubjectively constituted is irrelevant for the hermeneutics of subjectivity.

What I term the self-reflexivity of the subject is an interplay of reflection and self-reflection. A person makes use of the cultural language of intersubjectivity for self-understanding on the one hand, and they make use of their own self-understanding to accept or reject single practices, norms and rules that have been condoned by the prevalent language of culture on the other. The moral implications of the interplay of reflection and self-reflection are manifold. I will mention only the most important ones. The danger of empty subjectivism and relativism can be averted under the condition of a kind of reflection that, in my book *General Ethics*,[3] I have termed 'double-quality reflection'. Reflection becomes 'double-quality reflection' when persons distinguish between concrete and abstract norms and when they keep the abstract norms as a moral authority even if they reject the concrete norms as null and void. This issue would be of prime importance if we were examining the distinction between 'good' and 'bad' emotions. However, the juxtaposition of emotional wealth and poverty is a completely different matter, at least on the theoretical plane. The devil is certainly an emotionally poor creature. Evil normally appears in the shape of a person with strong but indifferentiated impulses or of a cold person who is capable of bringing manipulative–calculative logic to perfection. The emotionally rich person, on the other hand, may remain morally infantile or irresponsible unless they cultivate their moral sensibilities more than others.

Subjectivity as self-reflexivity opens up a treasure-trove of potentials for emotional differentiation. The person becomes the hermeneut of their own emotions. Of course, hermeneutics is neither a subcase of observation nor that of self-knowledge alone. In interpreting their emotions, in putting them under hermeneutic scrutiny, the person creates 'the emotional palette' of different shades of that particular emotion. This is certainly not creation but, as mentioned, interpretative differentiation. Given that the interpretation is inherent in the feeling quality itself, one or another shade of the palette will be *felt* in subsequent contact with other men, children, books, flowers, or anything else. The tension between the (relative) poverty of emotional language and the richness of feelings themselves will make itself felt. Solution of the tension could be sought in two directions. First, one can try to adapt the language to the self-differentiation of feelings and, second, one can try to stop the self-reflective differentiation of emotions and attempt to regain emotions that are, once again from the perspective of subjectivity, strong, fundamental and undifferentiated. Once the split between emotional terms and personal–emotional differentiation widens into an abyss, the differentiated self of emotional sensitivity becomes incommunicado. Incognito (in Kierkegaard's sense), solipsism, madness are, at least in my view, no general options.

III

Let us suppose that in a group of people everyone cultivates their own emotions, sensibilities and sentiments. This group of people can establish among themselves a kind of *culture* that institutionalizes, so to speak, emotional cultivation. After all, one can cultivate emotional density collectively. The shared language of an emotional culture like this can be the language of art, as Hegel pointed out, in particular the language of painting, poetry and music. In addition, new gestures, ceremonies, a completely new, esoteric world of signs can be inserted into the common language of signs as the very network of interpretation of differentiated significations. If one is the member of a group like this, one will certainly perceive the absence of the same or similar emotional culture in others as the manifestation of utter emotional impoverishment, and not without reason.

This scenario is far from hypothetical, it is real. This is exactly what happened in the eighteenth and nineteenth centuries. Certain groups of the bourgeoisie, the bourgeoisified aristocracy and the gentry indeed developed an esoteric culture of emotional refinement and self-cultivation. It is certain groups, and not the bourgeoisie or the gentry *in toto*, that are under discussion. An esoteric culture is by definition one of separation where the act of separation implies a claim to superiority, albeit not necessarily of social superiority and privilege. Cultural superiority is rather a tool to compensate for social inferiority. Cultural differentiation with the claim of cultural superiority requires the cultivation of ways of life that do not, or do not entirely, match the general lifestyle of the class within the framework of which it emerges.

The subjectivity of a modern person can put its cachet on many a thing, and it can open up diverse fields of possibilities for itself. The venture of emotional differentiation is only one of them. The cultivation of sensitivity is esoterism with the flavour of cultural opposition. The emotionally rich person despises possessive individu-alism, and has nothing but contempt for the businessman, the petty bourgeois, the politician. The oppositional drive is perhaps the main driving force behind the cultivation of sensitivity, for it requires introspection, which in turn requires leisure, freedom from the ordinary business of life. A ceremonial emotional culture in fact segregates.

At the same time, the central category of emotional self-cultivation is wealth. The millionaire and the bohemian artist are equally 'wealthy', the only difference being that their wealth consists of different coinage. The wealth of money is external, that of sensitivity is internal. A person and their money are different, and this wealth can be lost. A person and their sensitivity are identical – the person *is* the bundle of their emotions and sentiments, and this cannot be taken from them. Furthermore, the millionaire's wealth has been created not by him but by others (in terms of nineteenth-century socialism: by the proletariat). However, an esoteric person's (emotional) wealth is created by the person and it cannot be taken away from them. Money is alienated and alienable, so is political power or fame. In contrast, emotional density or wealth are analienable. In terms of this vision, there is a dirty, alienated and inferior kind of wealth, and there is one that is shining and non-alienated – and this is the real one.

The nineteenth century spoke the language of wealth and poverty, and Marx was no exception to this. Communism ensures the appropriation of the wealth of the species by every individual; the ideal is the person rich in needs and, needless to say, rich in its emotional culture. Scarcity was for the nineteenth century a heavily negative term, the shame or the dark side of the existence of the human race. The cultivators of sensitivity failed to notice that the spectre of scarcity made its appearance amidst them as well.

The dialectics of cultivation became progressively perceived. I will exemplify this development with an abstract model rather than with the analysis of historical processes. As is well known, the person faces, having differentiated their emotional world, the dilemma of communicability. It is precisely this dilemma that seems to be solved by creating a special, esoteric culture for the cultivation of sensibility, including of course artistic sensibilities. The creation of such a network of esoteric cultural signs does sublate the contradiction but only under one condition: the original normative framework of behaviourial patterns, duties and rights must remain intact and the esoteric cultivation of sentiments must be practised within this broader framework, thus composing an esoteric niche within a broader, established way of life. However, once the binding character of the socio-political intersubjective norms and rules vanishes, and only the esoteric sign-world of the ceremonies of sensibilities remains, the person, the carrier of this sensibility, will be cut off from the network of the active participant members of the society in which they dwell. The private world of esoterics will further be protected by the broader world; those submerged exclusively in the cultivation of sensibilities rarely earn their daily bread. It is in this respect that Thomas Mann mentions *machtgeschutzte Innerlichkeit* (inwardness shielded by power). Submerged in their hypercultivated sensitivities, these overrefined plants of the European soil fail to notice, or choose not to notice, the glass roof protecting them from an early frost. Moreover, they increasingly despise the outer frosty world of the insensitive, 'dull' masses.

Men and women relate reflectively to the world of political–social norms, institutions, rights and obligations in so far as they re-cast and reactivate them while acting within their frameworks, and reject those that cannot be condoned by their conscience. As long as they re-cast and reactivate these norms, as long as they go about their everyday and non-everyday practical business together with their fellow creatures, they have to make choices. However, in an active life there are major commitments and minor commitments, there are life-long as well as merely temporal preferences. *Therefore there is a hierarchy and not just a difference*. This hierarchy is not social in nature, nor is it, though it may be, the internalization of social hierarchy. Yet it is a value hierarchy in a double sense of the word. One can ask the question: which value is preferred to which other one? One can also ask the question: which thing, person, activity or profession of *value* is more precious for me, for my personality? In a scenario like this the 'old' distinctions between particular emotions maintain their relevance. Deep emotions are steady, constant, essential. They are not just one among several emotional shades, they stand out, they steer and sometimes even compel us. Superficial sentiments, on the other hand, are vested into insignificant matters. They can wither, and we will not miss them if they disappear from the palette. Certain emotions are strong if the situation so requires and weak if it does not. Certain sentiments are strong while others are weak. Not all of our sensibilities are of equal relevance; one can cultivate some and neglect others. This is not a scenario of less subjectivity but one of less subjectivism. This is the scenario I call 'the emotional household'. Like every household, this too copes with scarcity. This is a scenario of subjectivity, because it is precisely the person who has to learn to cope with the limitedness of their own emotional resources and use them properly, with good measure, in accordance with their obligations and desires. This is a scenario of less subjectivism because one manages a household (including an emotional household) for others as well as for oneself as being related to others. The cultivation of sensibility is a constituent of a household like this, but one that has to be kept in its right proportion.

Subjectivity is the condition of differentiation of emotions and of the cultivation of emotional sensibility. The cult of sensibility had its finest hour *ante rem*, in *Clarissa, Werther, Marianne*. Whereas *ex post facto*, that is, after the Napoleonic wars, the selfsame cult started to display its more problematic face. From Flaubert's *Sentimental Education* to Proust's *'temps perdu'*, the infinite wealth of the shades of feeling begin to destroy the personality itself. The cult of sensibility finally culminates in Musil's *Man without Qualities*.[4] If one endlessly continues to differentiate one's own emotional life, refinement finally becomes so subtle, so manifold, elastic, vacillating and ephemeral that nothing that is steady has been retained: no personal quality persists. And yet the person of an esoteric culture remains the person of this particular culture. The ceremonies of sensitivity remain intact, whilst the subjectivity disappears behind them. What remains is the discourse itself: the discourse of esoterism.

IV

When Stendhal's hero, Fabrizio del Dongo, toys with the idea after Waterloo of trying his luck in America, his aunt, the princess Sanseverina, mockingly asks the rebellious youth whether he could imagine himself living 'in the democracy of merchants'. The answer is obviously negative. 'The democracy of merchants' is repulsive not because it is a democracy; Sanseverina would have no difficulties relocating her refined nephew in the age of Pericles. But for this kind of subjectivity merchants are rude, banausic, uncultivated, prosaic. They have neither taste nor good manners. The great-grandchildren of similar 'merchants' in Western, Southern and Central Europe followed the tradition of Stendhal's heroes: they held everything popular in contempt. The sole exception was *le peuple*, the mythological People or the proletariat writ large. They were the heirs-designate of a fading culture. Lukács did not need to indulge in projecting the disappearance of the esoteric bourgeois subject onto the emerging mass society. He could afford openly to denounce the overrefinement of the esoteric–aesthetic culture. The price he paid for it was his enthusiastic appeal to the new barbarians who, while tearing to pieces the ceremonial ties of an already subjectless world, would supposedly reintroduce grandeur, individuality and subjectivity along with strong emotions and a thriving new culture. For the time being, only the premise of this prediction has come true. The cultural threads of an overrefined world have been torn to pieces, yet no individuality, heroism or authentic personality has emerged, only naked barbarism. Yet this unhappy historical development cannot be taken as proof of the emotional impoverishment of modern, i.e. 'herd', man.

'Impoverishment' is a relative term: it means 'poorer than previously'. An impoverished man of material wealth can still be fairly well off, but the term 'emotional impoverishment' carries strong negative connotations. If one compares the post-modern person with the high priests of the cult of emotional refinement, the 'emotional impoverishment' detected in the post-modern person does not necessarily indicate merely a loss of value. For one could imagine men and women making up for the loss of certain emotional shades through greater emotional depth and an intelligent emotional household. In what follows I shall use the term 'emotional impoverishment' only when the absence of emotional differentiation is accompanied by emotional superficiality. 'Emotional impoverishment' occurs when the dominant emotional language turns banal, and when there is no sign of any alternative imaginary institutions of signification that might induce emotional refinement or sensibilities.

When it comes to the criticism of 'one-dimensionality', mass culture, mass media and mass technology are normally the prime targets, the assumption being that the industrial mass production of records, record players and television sets is responsible for cultural decay and the impoverishment of emotional life. I have tried to prove that such and similar accusations should be viewed with a grain of scepticism. The accusers are in fact the great-grandchildren of Fabrizio del Dongo, people highly suspicious of 'masses' and 'merchants'. They are also the ones who project their own experiences to the loss of subject amidst overrefinement onto a world that is alien to them. To set the story straight: in this atmosphere, emotional terms and expressions become suspect and they first lose ground in the 'high' culture at a time when they still capture the imagination and continue to linger on in the 'low' culture. Actually, it was Musil who pointed out this development in the theoretical chapters of *Man without Qualities*. Emotional refinement emptied out the emotional expressions themselves. If shades of emotion can no longer be communicated in direct speech, it stands to reason that traditional emotional terms, those vehicles of direct communication, turn banal. And since a well-refined person cannot be 'banal', they must shy away from using traditional emotional terms. 'Shy away' is not a metaphor. Overrefined persons are actually deeply ashamed of using 'common' emotional expressions. Since their subjectivity becomes manifest not in action, moral resoluteness or behaviour, but rather only in their own sensibility, they are afraid of losing this subjectivity by using 'common' emotional terms. An overrefined person is less afraid of denouncing his neighbour than of talking banalities. 'Common' emotional terms are banned as 'banal', thus the language of the cult of refinement will be emptied of such expressions. To turn to someone and simply say, 'I love you', becomes ridiculous, banal and therefore emotionally prohibited.

At the same time, the mass media continued to produce their one-line emotionalism ('I love you' – 'I love you too'); and occasionally they still produce such texts. Emotional expressions swamped the lyrics and music of popular culture. But it could not for long resist the trends that came through the filter of high culture faster than ever. Popular culture soon began to contribute to the anti-sentimentalist drive. Finally everyone became ashamed of using a straightforward emotional language, everyone began to feel that this language is 'banal'. However, without an emotional language, including the language of sentiments, even the ingredients of an emotional household will be in short supply. Although emotional terms are merely forms and frameworks, yet it is within such forms and frameworks that sensibility develops and blossoms. If the form, the framework is absent, emotional impoverishment in the strictest sense of the word follows. Emotional impoverishment does not mean the absence of emotions, it rather means the absence of emotional refinement, and it does mean the absence of sentiments. It is tantamount to the absence of emotional culture, of sensibility. Although people in 'real' life still use emotional expressions, sometimes even lavishly, the anti-sentimentalist drive, which has conquered the world of contemporary imagination for the moment, does not provide much support to a sensibility-oriented emotional household.

One can, of course, tell a different story, insisting that men and women in modern life no longer need emotional refinement in their daily life. Subjectivity is after all a luxury. Men and women perform functions in a variety of institutions and they develop merely functional relations to their fellow creatures. Functional relationships of this kind do not call for emotional differentiation. Sentiments are not only superfluous, they are also dangerous. It was after all the sentiment of love that enslaved women to men in an epoch when objectively they could have already become free. As far as the enjoyment of works of art is concerned, we enjoy them with ears and eyes, not with sentiments. To develop a special sensibility termed taste is superfluous. Tastes are anyway subjective or, alternatively, they are totally manipulated. If this is our viewpoint of appraisal, the disappearance of emotional expressions and patterns from 'high' as well as 'low' culture can be accounted for by the reflection theory or by the theory of 'homology'. High and low culture only reflect what is going on in 'life' or, in another rendering, the disappearance of emotional language from most of our media is homologous with the disappearance of emotions from 'life', or with the modern trend of putting a premium on this disappearance. This story could explain the phenomenon that emotional expressions and terms are really felt, and in fact are banal. For what is felt to be banal is banal. We have no other criteria for assessing banality.

It is possible to speak a cultural language that is far from conducive to the emotional sensibility of the human person, one that is nevertheless capable of guiding men and women in their everyday life. An example of this is the language of 'health versus sickness'. One can discuss calories, headaches, heartbeats and exercises in the same way that others discuss love, friendship, the colour of the sky, the modulation of a voice, with the difference that talk of health will not differentiate one's subjectivity although it will sharpen one's sense of observation (of one's own body). A personal household of health is as much possible as an emotional household. Scarcity is characteristic of both. Yet whereas a well-conducted household results in the first case in 'personality quality', it results in the second case in a 'bodily quality'. Obviously the 'discourse on the body' so widespread in recent years is only partly a liberating act from the soul-body dualism. It also serves as a spearhead pointing at the 'heart', which is a well-known metaphor for emotions. This spearhead can, however, turn into a boomerang.

But I would still stake my bet on the reappearance of emotional culture, or rather on the appearance of several emotional cultures. Bodies are not differentiated enough, they are not even sufficiently erotic if they lack the appeal that can only be conferred on them by emotional differentiation. What can be new and at the same time different? Only emotional refinement, which, once again, can become new and which is by definition different.

Notes

1 I refer readers to my book, *A Theory of Feelings* (The Hague: Van Gorcum, 1979), where I properly distinguish between 'emotion', 'sentiment' and their subgroups which are all 'feelings'.
2 Aristotle, *Rhetoric*, 1379a 1o.
3 A. Heller, *General Ethics* (Oxford: Blackwell, 1988).
4 Robert Musil, *Man without Qualities*, translated by Eithne Wilkens and Ernst Kaiser (London: Pan, 1988).

5
What Is Practical Reason and What Is It Not?

I

The new upsurge in the Heidegger debate reopened the question whether certain philosophies or philosophers can be held morally or politically responsible for the gravest collective crimes of modern history. Discussants used the opportunity to explore the general issue of the relation between philosophy and morals, theoretical reason and practical reason. A recent German publication with the title *Destruction of the moral self-consciousness: opportunity or danger?*[1] addresses the above problems in a very wide framework. I have therefore chosen this book as the starting point for my present reflections.

Two papers, written by philosophical adversaries (Karl-Otto Apel and Otto Poggeler, respectively), deserve special attention. Apel's study raises the question 'Could we have learned something specific from the national catastrophe?'[2] and promises to proceed in an autobiographical manner. It soon becomes apparent that by autobiography Apel means the description of his philosophical development from existential philosophy to transcendental pragmatics. Obviously, the personal pronoun 'we' of the title (could *we* have learned something. . .) refers not to German men and women but to German philosophers. The lesson German philosophers could or should draw from the 'national catastrophe' is to accept transcendental pragmatism, the only modern universalistic philosophy that is, and can possibly be. For Apel, philosophy is not a game to be confined within the walls of the academy, not an exercise in mere problem-solving, but a vocation of the highest dignity and the highest moral responsibility. It is out of this conviction that he rejects all contemporary philosophies of a non-universalistic bent as morally suspect and 'conservative'.

Otto Poggeler[3] discusses Heidegger's philosophy and demonstrates, in my mind correctly, that ethics (practical philosophy) could not have been completely fitted into Heidegger's vision at any stage of his development. But this theoretical reflection immediately assumes some strange practical relevance for Poggeler. Heidegger's well-known reluctance to take moral responsibility for his participation in the Nazi movement is now to be explained by the absence of ethics in his philosophy.

Though divided by a theoretical abyss, the papers by Apel and Poggeler are complementary, given that both see a direct connection between a personal moral stance and philosophy. Something more is involved here than the traditional injunction that a philosopher should live in the spirit of his own philosophy. Apel insists that a philosopher should have a philosophy that offers him and the world proper moral guidance. Poggeler speculates that, if one's philosophy does not offer such guidance (as in Heidegger's case), one cannot be held responsible, as a person, for not living according to common moral principles.

The volume could have been edited by Puck, for it contains, as the last paper, the well-known essay by Richard Rorty on the primary of democracy as against philosophy.[4] It seems as if this practical joke allows the reader to make a clean sweep of almost all the serious claims and counter-claims, accusations and counter-accusations that happen to fill 272 pages. Rorty's level-headed writing comes as a wholesome counter-balance against absolutist and fundamentalist philosophical ambitions, yet it rests on shaky foundations. Unlike Apel and Poggeler, who, albeit with different value preferences, erroneously equate practical reason with philosophy and practical philosophy with practical reason, Rorty, in a haphazard and overzealous gesture, denies that there is *any* relevant connection between them.

The ethico-political neutrality of philosophical systems, language games and principles results, according to Rorty, from the fact that liberal democracy does not call for philosophical legitimation. To this idea I would object that among all the forms of governance *only* liberal democracy has so far called for philosophical legitimation. (The pre-modern forms of governance were legitimated by traditions, myths and religions and not by philosophies, whereas totalitarian societies and states claim to be legitimated by sciences, and are actually legitimated by charisma or tradition.) Active legitimating practices are never continuous; they are mobilized only in cases of acute or chronic legitimation deficiency. Since liberal democracies are constantly exposed to philosophical and ideological attack, the absence of philosophical legitimation can contribute to the demise of the ethico-political bonds of the civic commonwealth. And it would be difficult to deny that Hegel had a point: the very existence, the so-called 'positivity', of institutions is but an empty shell unless supported by the ethical practice of people committed to them. The German experience must not be dismissed so lightheartedly, after all. And even if Rorty were right, and all philosophies become politically neutral, they could not possibly be neutral towards one another. The moment philosophers cease to detect the dangerous elements in the philosophy of others, the genre itself is going to disappear, for what will remain is just another chess game, jigsaw puzzle or crossword puzzle, a mere formal mental exercise of minor importance and interest.

II

Works of art rarely turn to one another; they have no dispute with one another; they do not exclude one another; they are neither friendly nor unfriendly towards each other. Be they classical, modern or post-modern, they stand alone and they do not care whether there are others like them. Cold stars that bring warmth to alien lives, they are but mirror images of our existential solitude. Works of philosophy are different. They constantly challenge one another; they argue, discuss, advise, denounce; they exclude and include others; they are friendly and unfriendly; they love and hate; this is how they become the mirror images of our unsocial sociability. Our life experiences manifest themselves both in the world of works of art and in the world of philosophy. All other arguments aside, we do a disservice to philosophy when we treat works of philosophy as if they were works of art. We are never in total accord with our fellow creatures; we can never entirely consent to their opinions. Philosophies that do not fight with one another cannot be the mirror images of our unsocial sociability. No hierarchy (between artworks and philosophical works) is suggested here, no judgement is passed on any single work. What was said has been said in defence of the genre called philosophy. If one wants to have philosophies one cannot have them as neutral entities, one cannot have them as beautiful flowers just growing in the garden of a benevolent but indifferent liberal democracy. But the plea for universal consensus does not fare any better either, because where there is universal consensus about a universal consensus (even if this is restricted to the foundation of all our norms, moral norms included) there is no more philosophy left because there is no *fundamental* thing to disagree and to fight about.

Philosophies are always on collision course, but philosophers do not need to be. The adversary is not the enemy. What my philosophy excludes, I (as a person) do not need to exclude. I may even like the work that has been excluded by mine on many counts: I can enjoy it aesthetically, praise it ethically, agree with it politically, or simply find it interesting. Furthermore, I can sympathize (or not) with the author of a work irrespective of the relation between our works. Relativism is neither liberal nor democratic – and it is certainly aphilosophical. The attitude to a work and to the author of the work need not be conflated into one. Goethe once said that *ideas should not be tolerant, but the attitude, 'the mind' (Gemut) should be*. In philosophy, things can carry on just as they mostly do in everyday life or in public life: we can have allies who are not our best friends, while some of our friends will not share many of our opinions and judgements.

I take it to be self-evident that decent persons will not have indecent people as personal friends. As we know from experience, a person who is committed to values we believe to be right, and who (in our view) holds a few just opinions about public matters, can still be a scoundrel, and vice versa. Is it the ethics of the philosopher one needs to share or have something in common with, or the ethics supposedly inherent in (or lacking from) the philosophy itself?

If there is no tension (or even practical contradiction) between the message of a philosophy on the one hand, and the character (or action) of the philosopher on the other, there are no difficulties to face. Such is the case with Rosenberg, who was sentenced to death by the standards of natural right. Although I am not a friend of the brand of utilitarianism that makes a case for the execution of innocent tourists if the 'greatest happiness of the greatest numbers' so requires, I can remain the friend of the (personally liberal and charitable) man who makes such and similar statements.

It is easiest to exemplify the other extreme by Heidegger's case. Heidegger's philosophy definitely does not 'contain' any Nazism, though it has a strong affinity to all brands of extreme radicalism. This time a great philosopher behaved as a moral scoundrel. I do not even say that he *was* one, but he certainly behaved like one, for he failed to take responsibility for his actions (not for his philosophy). Taking moral responsibility is to respond truthfully. Cain's answer to God's question, 'Where is your brother Abel?' ('Am I my brother's keeper?'), is the archetype of the wrong response (Cain does not take responsibility). This was also Heidegger's response. Instead of answering truthfully ('I have belonged to those who have murdered my brother Abel'), he repeated both with unmistakable allusions and with his silence the spurious question of responsibility-avoidance: 'Am I my brother's keeper?' Has philosophy anything to do with such an elementary case of moral incompetence? Actually, one cannot establish any positive, thetic, connection between Heidegger's philosophy and his moral incompetence. The Nazis did not even use Heidegger for their own ends (similarly, the Bolsheviks never used Lukács), and I think that they were better judges in such matters than our contemporaries who feverishly try to pinpoint such connections. It was rather Nietzsche's philosophy that the Nazis used, and, if my judgement of character is worth anything, Nietzsche would have been the last to become a Nazi. I think that it was rather the taboo on revoking an existential choice that was decisive in Heidegger's case, because it immunized him against ethical responsibility, as existential choices always do, except if the ethical itself has been existentially chosen. It is certainly possible to remain a friend of Heidegger's philosophy and to pass serious moral judgement on his actions and his character, which I am inclined to do, just as it is possible to show hostility to Heidegger's philosophy, if this is what follows from one's position in the network of unsocial sociability. But there is neither philosophical nor moral foundation for the practice of drawing certain, too general, conclusions from this single case – a coincidence of many heterogeneous factors – about some necessary connections between certain philosophies and certain kinds of public or private morals. Too many 'unsocial' elements in the game of unsocial sociability are not to be counted as a moral credit either.

III

Fundamentalist enemies have never tired of denouncing philosophy as a dangerous enterprise (dangerous to the state, to religion, and to morals in particular). Yet the friends of philosophy and philosophers themselves have frequently entertained similar ideas. Plato, the first to discover that evil maxims rather than evil impulses destroy the moral foundations of political life, tried hard to blame the enemies of philosophy (rhetors and sophists) for disseminating those evil maxims; but he too had to warn the youth off from his own philosophy, for even the most sublime philosophy, if misunderstood, can lead them astray. There are two typical modern approaches to this question, the Kantian and the Hegelian. In proposing a straightforward dualism (between metaphysics of nature and metaphysics of morals) Kant declared the whole territory of theoretical philosophy (philosophy of nature in a broad understanding) adiaphoric, and the whole territory of practical philosophy moral. In the theoretical pursuit nothing can be forbidden and nothing should be declared dangerous, unless the theoretical pursuit contradicts the universal moral law as provided by practical philosophy. Hegel, on the other hand, cut the ties between morals and philosophy altogether. Not only one or the other philosophy is dangerous, he insisted in his lectures on *History of Philosophy*, but philosophy is altogether a dangerous enterprise.[5] Whenever one embarks on doing philosophy one needs to take this simply into account.

Let us assume together with Hegel that philosophy is a morally and politically dangerous enterprise. Hegel did not make exceptions (such as one kind of philosophy is dangerous, another kind is not), because he assumed that every serious philosophy is dangerous, or at least can be used in a dangerous manner; so do I.

Philosophy once had a bad reputation because those who practised it took intellectual delight in upsetting everyday knowledge and intuition, traditional beliefs and time-honoured customs. This seems not to be our problem anymore. In modernity the philosophical procedure has become everyday practice. We are constantly upsetting traditional practices and moral institutions in our daily life and in the political arena alike. The problem with philosophy is no longer procedural, but *substantive*. Not *that* it upsets moral intuitions, but *what* kind of moral intuitions it upsets, not *that* it ridicules time-honoured customs but *what* kind of time-honoured customs it exposes to derision become the source of danger. To be precise: the problem with philosophy is not that it makes wrong suggestions or fails to make the right ones, but that it simply makes all its suggestions (whatever they are) look proper and right; moreover, it makes them just right within the framework of the particular philosophy that presents the suggestion. This is as much true about anti-metaphysics as about metaphysics. There is an attraction in the attitude of pure speculation that can be called demonic, for the power that can make everything just look right or true is a demonic power.

Hegel's standpoint (to which I also subscribe) sounds bizarre. After all, philosophy is taught in much-respected academic institutions, sometimes as a kind of history – where excellence is measured by the number of footnotes – sometimes as a mental exercise – where excellence is measured by the skill for discovering inconsistencies in others and replacing them with new ones. This is all very respectable and completely harmless. And it is the continuation of some of the oldest traditions of the genre. There is nothing demonic about philosophy if it is learned and absorbed as a whole, if the results are learned together with the arguments that led up to them, and if all arguments are presented in the setting in which they originally appeared, in their proper context. I have termed the result of such a learning process the total (complete) reception of a philosophy. If someone is a total recipient, they learn exactly *how* a statement has assumed truth and correctness within the context of a philosophy; they also acquire the skills to refute such claims to truth (if they so wish) by putting questions and answers into a different context. Making all things look right in the framework in which they look right is a sheer speculative activity. To abandon ourself to pure speculation is an entirely adiaphoric pastime, at least for modern men and women. Slipping into the skin of a philosophy and dwelling therein is neither good nor evil, neither right nor wrong from the moral point of view. But if this is true, and it would be hard to deny that it is, how could we possibly believe that to think up a new philosophy is to be subjected to moral judgement? Since I do not subject my neighbour to moral censure for being a Marxist, a Heideggerian or a follower of Nietzsche, what justifies me in passing moral judgements on the *maîtres penseurs* themselves for having conceived one of those philosophies?

The total reception of a philosophy is the philosophical reception proper. It continues in a series of interpretations and reinterpretations, which all remain on the speculative level. But the reception of philosophy rarely remains merely speculative. Moreover, the more significant a philosophy is, the less the reception of the philosophy remains solely on the speculative plane. All the total receptions of philosophy, in all subsequent interpretations, are surrounded by the partial reception of the same philosophy, as the planet Saturn is surrounded by its rings. Partial reception can be aesthetic, scientific, ethical or political. But, whatever kind it is, partial recipients use philosophy for non-philosophical purposes, be they theoretical, pragmatic or practical. On the speculative plane, philosophies transform all statements into right (true) statements *of* a particular philosophy; in the process of partial reception, however, these statements are torn from their speculative context and placed into a completely different, sometimes practical, one, with the pretension of remaining as true and right in this new (practical) context as they were in the original (speculative) one. It is at this point that philosophy can become dangerous. And this happens not without the active contribution of philosophers themselves. Philosophers have always been desirous of partial reception and, even after the withering of the idea of the philosopher-king, they still remained. A philosophy that can never become dangerous is worthless, for it is a philosophy that never attracted the attention and the enthusiasm of partial recipients.[6]

Thus we arrive at the paradox that it is only through partial reception that philosophy can become dangerous, but that without partial reception(s) a philosophy is just a kind of crossword puzzle. We also arrive at the second paradox that philosophy, as a mere speculative activity, is entirely adiaphoric. Yet philosophy is used in practice too, where it can become dangerous; in addition, philosophers are desirous of the partial reception of their philosophy. Philosophers like to live dangerously, yet at the same time plead innocence, so it seems. However, philosophers are rarely aware of their own paradoxical situation, for at least two reasons.

The first reason is related to the qualification of being dangerous. Being dangerous to what? Being dangerous to whom? Questions like these can always be raised. Philosophers are desirous for practical application, for they want to be dangerous to the evil, to the wrong, to the dangerous. Whoever is dangerous to the dangerous is innocent. This is far from being a false pretension by definition. Philosophy can be dangerous to evil forces, to ideological lies, to despots, to tyrants and thus to philosophers themselves. It can also be dangerous to self-indulgence, to self-righteousness, to political blindness, to repression, to oppression, to moral decay. Yet philosophy can also be dangerous to equality, human dignity, democracy, moral intuitions, practical rationality, and much else. Philosophy can be dangerous to all kinds of prejudices and prejudgements, be they right or wrong.

Second, from the standpoint of philosophy, all philosophies *but one* are, by definition, untrue. It is self-evident, then, that practices supported by those – untrue – philosophies will be morally dangerous and politically suspect. Yet since one's own philosophy is right, and the only right one, one cannot help being desirous of its partial reception. If only one's own philosophy were broadly accepted and followed, everything would turn out right; or at least the gravest dangers would be avoided. And if they are not, other philosophers will be put on the stand.

IV

Accusing one another of making mischief is, on the one hand, a punch below the belt, for it is not the philosopher who actually does the mischief but the partial recipient of the philosophy. The accusation is, on the other hand, quite justified. Though philosophers inherit their medium, and with the medium a typical Question and Answer kit, they also know before embarking on the philosophical expedition what statements, claims, images, visions and intuitions need to be (or should be) made right (true) at the end of their speculative journey. Though the whirlwind of their own making can carry philosophers away, and open before them horizons of enquiry whose very existence they had no premonition of at the beginning of their expedition, the most decisive statements of their philosophies predate their philosophies. They are distilled from 'life', from 'practice'. For example, no moral philosopher has ever invented moral norms or maxims; they rather distilled them from life experiences, clarified them and finally put them into the context of their philosophy. No one was more perfectly aware of this circumstance than Kant himself, who grounded the pure idea of Freedom in everyday intuitions such as the existence of good persons and the voice of our conscience. This is why the well-known mutual accusations of philosophers are not entirely punches below the belt. They well know the game they are playing. The recipients, so they argue, can take out from the bag only what the philosopher put into it in the first place.

There is, actually, nothing morally wrong in blaming *philosophies* for some practical mischief in addition to their speculative shortcomings, which remain always the main targets. Anyway, from a philosophical point of view, the two aspects cannot be totally disentangled. As long as the attacks remain exercises in speculation, the same must be said about them as about all kinds of philosophical speculation: they are adiaphoric. As long as one merely speculates, one continues to dwell in an adiaphoric homogeneous medium. Yet the moment one starts to attack the *philosopher* (the author) together with his philosophy, one leaves the homogeneous medium of speculation and behaves as an actor to whom the same moral norms apply as to every other actor. Let me enumerate only a few, such as: one should care for the other person's sensibility, one should respect the other person's autonomy, one should pass fair judgements. It is completely irrelevant from the moral point of view that the actors (the person who passes value-judgements on another person's character or action and the person whose character and actions are to be judged) happen to be a partial or total recipient of different philosophies and that they have acted or do act in such a capacity. This qualification cuts both ways. Even if a philosopher deserves moral recrimination, the just moral judgement cannot be extended to their philosophy, for doing philosophy is and remains a merely speculative and thus adiaphoric enterprise. Lastly, since to reject or to criticize a philosophy by pointing at the dangers that have eventuated or might eventuate from its reception is also a merely speculative exercise, and thus adiaphoric, one cannot claim merits in practising criticism like this. To put the moral shortcomings of others under critical scrutiny is not a virtue unless the author exposes himself to negative sanctions in and because of doing so. In the latter case, it is not the right opinion that will be morally credited but civic courage – moral virtue. Right opinion is just *recta ratio* in theoretical reasoning, in both its philosophical or its everyday use.

Even if a morally and politically foolproof philosophical theory were possible (which I do not believe), it could not be completely shielded from dangerous reception. What follows here is meant as a qualified criticism of Kant's refutation of the celebrated common saying that what is true in theory is still irrelevant in practice. The attempt to make security foolproof always backfires because in real life nothing is morally foolproof, and never will be. One can find the single principle to rely upon in practice at the level of speculation, but in actual practice the principle will still fail to offer secure guidance in our most momentous decisions. This is why even the philosophy that does its utmost to be morally foolproof can end up becoming dangerous when it comes to practical application.

Nothing exemplifies this quandary more than Kant's own philosophy. Secured a hundred times over, both morally and politically, his philosophy, too, can provide false, even evil, maxims – perhaps precisely because it is so overprotected. Let us start with the basics. The categorical imperative does not allow for any exceptions. Without such an absolute injunction, Kant's moral philosophy could not become consistent neither could its moral purity be protected against contamination. Yet Kant himself showed us how the absolute maxim of no exception can become evil if applied in practice. If there is no exception from telling the truth, then we ought to tell the prospective murderer that his intended victim is hiding in our house. (This murderer could be the agent of the secret police.) We should never rebel against a tyrant, for we cannot wish that rebellion should be a universal law. This we certainly cannot wish, and yet there are situations when we should rebel, and everyone who advises us to the contrary provides us with an argument for doing just the wrong thing. Kant is right in theory. His moral philosophy becomes subtle and conclusive because there are no exceptions to the moral law. How can there be an exception if there is a law? And yet: our moral intuitions suggest that, in practice, in certain situations, we should make exceptions, that we need to listen to our moral sense for the concrete, for the unique, for the kind of singular that cannot simply be subjected to the universal without moral offence. *Phronesis* still wields moral authority. To propose that it should not is just another dangerous philosophical recommendation, even if made with subtle moral intent.

I hope that none of my readers will conclude that I have joined the chorus of those who make Kant responsible for Auschwitz or the Gulag. Rather, I have said the opposite. Kant protected his philosophy from the danger of being plundered in search of evil maxims as far as it was humanly possible. (It takes far less effort to misuse Hobbes, Nietzsche, even Hegel than to misuse Kant in this manner.) What I wanted to show is rather that no philosophy of great format can be completely sheltered from being so used. Whatever one does with one's philosophy one cannot exclude the danger of its being used for purposes unintended in the philosophical corpus itself.

After this short detour let me stress once more that philosophy, as an exercise in speculation, is adiaphoric. No one takes moral responsibility in doing philosophy. But philosophy is also dangerous – to become (somehow) dangerous is one of the foreseeable consequences that ensue from the very existence of philosophy. It is an elementary moral intuition that men and women carry moral responsibility for the foreseeable consequences of their actions. Philosophy is neither a man nor a woman; it is not a person, but an objectivation. As such it does not carry any responsibility – moral or non-moral. But the philosopher, as an author, is also a person; and as a person he or she could, or rather should, carry (moral) responsibility for the foreseeable consequences of what she or he does.

V

It is foreseeable that philosophy could be used in a dangerous way. What is not foreseeable, however, is whether it will actually be used in such a way or not. Furthermore, it is not foreseeable, or never completely so, for whom this philosophy will be dangerous, against what and in favour of what it will be (mis)used in the future. Let me repeat that philosophical ideas and maxims can bring havoc upon tyrants, despots and condescending ruling elites, they can play the role of the most formidable enemy of suicidal indifference and barbaric self-indulgence as much as they can undermine good moral intuitions and lend a helping hand to civilized barbarism and political corruption.

When speaking in consequentialist terms, we address the problem of prospective and not of retrospective responsibility. The issue here is not simply whether or not one is to be held responsible for certain consequences that have ensued from one's actions, but whether or not, before embarking on an action, one is obliged to gather information about, and take account of, all foreseeable consequences of one's action, and whether or not one should embark on a course of action *because* one has reason to expect only the most favourable consequences. However, both the strong and the weak version of consequentialism will agree on the issue of retrospective responsibility. Given that the consequences of an action could not possibly have been foreseen in advance, the actor cannot be held morally responsible for the results of their action. All philosophers can foresee that their language game is open to dangerous reception. But they cannot foresee to whom it might be and will be dangerous (in the future). To avoid the danger (in the spirit of strong consequentialism) would mean to avoid the genre. But once one avoids practising the genre, one ceases to be the author of *all* possible consequences of a world interpretation, and not just the bad ones. Actually, a philosopher cannot even know what (in his work) will be considered morally and politically beneficent or harmful in the future. Plato might perhaps have foreseen the collapse of his plans in Sicily, but he could not have had the slightest premonition that persecuted people in the twentieth century would find solace and moral edification in his Socratic dialogues.

Representative works of philosophy are practically immortal. So are representative philosophical tendencies, schools and vocabularies, even if the works that carry them are not. Strong consequentialism is irrelevant here for that reason alone. One cannot compare this story with that of the infinite chain of event-consequences, for the chain of consequences does not include direct access to the originating sources, whereas in philosophy it is precisely the originating action (the text) that is interpreted and reinterpreted *ad infinitum* (for all practical purposes). Interpreters can be entirely oblivious to the fact that interpretations of the same texts became embedded in events through partial reception, and, if so, when and how.

Let me repeat then that philosophers foresee very few of the eventual consequences of doing this or that kind of philosophy. From this it follows that a philosopher, as author, does not carry moral responsibility for the (future) reception of their philosophy. But what about the *foreseeable* consequences of their philosophy? Though philosophers are not (morally) responsible for doing philosophy, and the dangers ensuing therefrom, they can still be responsible for certain concrete dangers as follow because they could have foreseen certain concrete interpretations and partial receptions of their philosophy. The theoretical quandary with this proposition has already been indicated, namely that the 'chain of consequences' in philosophy is unlike the 'chain of events'. If one speaks about an initial action that enters the chain of events (and actions), foreseeable consequences and direct consequences mostly coincide (by direct I mean close both in space and in time). The foreseeable consequences are – normally – also the ones that directly follow from the act in question, whereas co-determining factors are sparse and also mostly well known. In philosophy this is otherwise. Direct consequences can ensue from the interpretation of texts two thousand years after their birth. Thus the foreseeable consequences (in philosophy) are not the sole direct, or necessarily the most momentous, ones. The problem can be eliminated only in Rorty's terms (philosophies are no longer dangerous because we live in a liberal democracy) provided that we are allowed to make true statements about the future (and we shall live in liberal democracies *ad infinitum*), which we certainly cannot.

Whenever and wherever the foreseeable consequences of an action are also the most direct consequences, one ought to take them into consideration before embarking on an action. If there is a strong likelihood of bad consequences ensuing, one should not embark on that action. But it is questionable whether the same can be said about a language game where the foreseeable and the most formidable (or the direct) do not coincide. Can I tell the philosopher, after his philosophy has been used to devise evil maxims, that since you could have – perhaps – foreseen this use you should have refrained from devising your philosophy (which is analogous to: you should not have embarked on this action)? This question is even more relevant to the case of Marx than to the case of Heidegger, and it should be answered in the negative, for all the reasons indicated above (the difference between the chain of events and the chain of interpretations).

Yet the moral intuition in favour of holding philosophers accountable for the eventual dangerous consequences of their philosophy is not entirely erroneous, because, where there is no prospective moral responsibility, retrospective responsibility can still be in force. Philosophers, as persons, can certainly be confronted with the morally and politically dangerous consequences of their philosophy that have occurred *in their lifetime*, if, and only if, they have failed to make a stand against the dangerous reception of their own philosophy because of vested interest, whether speculative, existential, political or some other. Taking responsibility, however, does not require the modification of the philosophy itself. Like a tragic hero who, when confronted with the dead bodies of his friends and enemies, exclaims in despair that this is not what he wanted, so the philosopher is duty bound to do likewise if similar situations occur. If they fail to do this, men and women have the reason and the right to believe that the philosopher actually wanted to be interpreted and used in the way they were. To deny the authenticity of one or another interpretation of a philosophy remains a matter of theoretical reason, but to deny the authenticity of a person who has failed to denounce the wrong as wrong and the evil as evil is a matter of practical reason. I mentioned previously that the common philosophical practice of denouncing the philosophy of others as morally dangerous is not a moral merit, whether right or wrong, unless civic courage is required for doing it. But it is always an act of courage to stand up against the dangerous interpretations of our own philosophy, especially if they are popular, and if standing up against them is dangerous to our own person and (or) position.

The kind of actions that philosophers should disallow in the use of their philosophy as a legitimating device (in their lifetime, of course) cannot be determined by a general moral norm. The threshold of moral toleration is decided rather by the moral and political conviction of the philosophers (as persons). Modern consciousness is dissatisfied whenever the threshold gives little scope for free interpretation. For us, this is fundamentalism, and, actually, it is. I would recommend the following maxim at this point: philosophers should protest against the use of their philosophy by partial recipients if they forge legitimating devices for genocide, mass murder and racism (if philosophers fail to do so, they carry moral responsibility for the consequences that ensue from the reception of their philosophy). This is a minimalist norm that I would recommend for more general application as the single common norm of the weakest possible ethos and I hope that it could be accepted. The principle of the weakest possible ethos replaces here the principle of consequentialism. Conscience suggests that the philosopher should protest on many other occasions and situations as well, but I do not dare to make a stronger recommendation. Here, as almost everywhere else, the final decision rests with the author/actor himself or herself. Here, as in so many other cases, one can still do the wrong thing by doing too little or doing too much – too much stands for fundamentalism, too little for moral irresponsibility and practical (not necessarily also philosophical) nihilism. The much-abused *phronesis* is thus the moral agency one needs to rely upon.

VI

Practical reason suggests what is the right thing (for us) to do. Conscience can be described as a moral feeling, the manifestation of our involvement in the suggestions of practical reason.

What we term 'practical reason' is, of course, not an empirical fact but a philosophical construct (an idea) that encompasses, and in a few philosophies also explains, the major personal and impersonal constituents of moral practice and attitude. Both moral intuitions (moral feelings) and norms (such as customs, general guidelines, imperatives, maxims, etc.) belong to the arsenal of moral constituents. Moral feelings are both motivational and mystical (gnostic), and norms, similarly, are both motivational and epistemic in character. In modern times, the epistemic aspect of moral norms has grown in importance, given that the authorization or validation of norms has become a major problem.

The dispute about the moral and political responsibility of philosophy is also a dispute about practical reason. Let us assume that all participants in the current debates wish to strengthen, if not the authority of practical reason, then at least the resoluteness of our resistance against genocide, mass murder and racism. Philosophers generally bet on one of three major moral constituents, which they entrust with the power to fend off the greatest moral dangers. One philosopher bets on universal norms and on universal procedures, the second on the institutions of liberal democracy, and the third puts his money on everyday moral intuitions. My proposition is that all three parties are certain losers, for the wager is the wrong one. Even if one bets on all three constituents, one can still end up a loser, although at least one stands a fair chance of winning. Let us take a very brief look at the three constituents.

Our moral intuitions are secondary, that is post-cognitive, as almost all of our intuitions are. One needs to be initiated into the meaning of a few moral images, concepts and attitudes, and to get into the practice of doing things according to moral expectations; only then can one develop moral intuitions. Thus, without moral norms there are no moral intuitions.

However, once developed, moral intuitions can prove more reliable moral guides than mere reasoning, especially if quick decisions need to be taken or in the most elementary moral situations. This is why Rousseau (among others) believed that pity is inborn and quasi-instinctual. It is a matter of fact that the sheer sensual impression of the suffering of a fellow creature affects our mind (or soul) with an elementary force, so much so that we feel the impulse to bring immediate relief to the sufferer. The original power of pity (and compassion) was not unknown to the main ideologues of totalitarianism. They regarded it as one of the most serious stumbling blocks to the realization of their projects. Maxims were invented to make people disregard the voice of pity, this sign of human weakness, which had to be heroically overcome and superseded. Instead of invoking moral monsters, I prefer to exemplify this connection with an anecdote about Lenin, who, as a person, was certainly not morally inferior to the human average. Lenin once said that he was afraid to listen to Beethoven's 'Appassionata' because the sonata enhanced in him the desire to caress people. Yet, he continued, we *should* beat people over the head, for our task is very difficult indeed. The story shows that the norm enjoins us to be pitiless, to overcome moral feelings.

The only innate moral feeling is shame, but the objects of shame (what we should be ashamed of) are learned. The elementary shame effect is extremely forceful when actions are performed within the radius of the regard of the members of one's community. We are ashamed before our neighbour, but we are less ashamed before unknown persons and in an unfamiliar environment. This is why it is, as a rule, easier to counterbalance the elementary affect of shame with bad or evil maxims once one leaves the boundaries of one's narrow environment, than to overcome feelings of compassion and of pity.

No unanimous conclusions can be drawn from the above observations. Or rather: one can draw many conclusions, but none of them will satisfy any of us.

Since a certain degree of conceptualization is a precondition of the development of elementary moral intuitions and since the objects of the shame affect are also socially (conceptually) given, the universalists have a point. Whether a person's moral sense will be a good moral sense depends in great part on the character of the norm or concept received at the very beginning of one's moral development. If one learns, for example, that only the members of one's caste feel the same pain as oneself, one will not extend the spontaneous feeling of pity to human beings beyond the pale of one's estate, unless one goes through a process of re-learning. The pain of a hound can strike the moral nerves of an aristocratic human far more than the pain of a socially inferior human creature. On the other hand, if we seriously considered accepting the thesis that only those moral norms are valid that have been established by rational discourse, we would certainly give up the sum total of our everyday moral intuitions. Since the devil argues well, moral intuitions can often put up greater resistance to evil than reasoning; it is easier to substitute evil maxims for good ones than to overcome good moral intuitions or moral feelings entirely. This is one of the reasons why it is so risky to undermine everyday intuitions (which grew out of traditions rather than rational discourse) and to ask them to show their moral licence, which is issued only to those who have already passed the examination at the universalistic grade.

Authors (and actors) who vest their full confidence in the institutions of liberal democracy have a good case as well. They could refer to the authority of Kant (if they so wished) that what is needed for the pursuit of decent politics is just good institutions, within whose framework even a race of devils would behave as decent persons. Yet Kant added to his doctrine of law a doctrine of virtues. Whatever our judgement of his doctrine may be, it certainly fills a place that is left empty by all theories of justice, in the present as much as in the past. The institutions of liberal democracy may offer the best framework for political choices and practices. But they do not provide a framework for forms of life. Here I return to Rorty's problem. It is a good thing that the state does not care much about our private morals, or even about our public virtues. But in the case of the total decomposition of a population's moral ties, such liberal–democratic institutions would not be perpetually reproducible. One can, of course, maintain that everyday moral intuitions, if untouched, will reproduce themselves anyway, but one cannot be so sure about this. Radical cultural critiques might have exaggerated, even over-exaggerated, the moral remissiveness and cultural decay of the (post-)modern world, but civilized barbarism is still not something one can so easily write off from the possibilities of contemporary history, our history.

There are modern persons who want to do the right thing. Wanting to do the right thing stands for 'being guided by practical reason as conscience'. The person who wants to do the right thing raises the question: 'What is the right thing for me to do?' Frequently there is no completely satisfactory answer to this question. But guidelines to the answer are provided by everyday intuitions, by universal norms and by the political practices of liberal democracies. Everyday intuitions for their part rely upon traditions such as empirical universals, local customs and religious and philosophical ideas, insights and practices, or rather upon the mixture of them all. A person who wants to do the right thing relies upon all three moral sources, albeit to different degrees, depending on their personal commitment, on their form of life, and also on the character of the moral problem they actually face.

It does not look either too simplistic or too difficult to try to elaborate a moral philosophy that borrows from and synthesizes all three ethical sources. But this is not the conclusion I wanted to arrive at in the framework of this particular essay.

VII

Let me sum up briefly a few preliminary conclusions first. Philosophy is adiaphoric, though it is also dangerous. Philosophers carry responsibility for the political and moral (mis)use of their philosophy during their lifetime, whether they speak up or remain silent about such (mis)use. To face the dangerous consequences of one's own philosophy is a practice of moral relevance, whereas to write against the dangerous consequences of the philosophy of others is common philosophical practice and, as such, adiaphoric.

Philosohers can know a hundred times over that philosophy is adiaphoric and they will still continue to denounce not only the theoretical shortcomings but (at least outside the walls of the academy) also the possible dangerous moral and political consequences of all other philosophies. This is the game we are playing. This is why philosophy is the mirror image of our unsocial sociability. Yet, I want to add something at this point. Philosohers are right and they have the right to criticize, to refute and to denounce each other in this way. This is because philosophy is actually a dangerous enterprise. Let me add to this that philosophy shares this feature with almost all other enterprises. But since philosophy pinpoints the danger in all the other enterprises, it is only just and fair that it does the same when it comes to its own language game. True enough, philosophers expose the dangers incipient in the philosophies of others, and not in their own, but, since all philosophers engage themselves in this enterprise, eventually all the possible (foreseeable) dangers incipient in all philosophies will be exposed and placed at the disposal of the recipient.

The three main conditions of reasonable politics and moral decency are, in principle, of equal weight, even if each of them is of greater weight in one particular situation and of lesser weight in another. Philosophies that make a strong case for any of the three provide a service. They also provide a service if they point out the possible dangers incipient in a philosophy that exalts only one of the three and neglects the other two. Given that partial recipients of a philosophy are mostly carried away by an 'absolute', it remains healthy, both morally and politically, to have access to alternatives, including the theoretical 'destruction' of their absolutes. Lastly, philosophers provide a great service if they understand how to step outside their philosophy as responsible (moral) persons and as citizens without giving up their absolute philosophical commitments.

As responsible (honest) persons and citizens, philosophers *must* step outside their own philosophy. They are then actors, moral and political agents, who cannot but be partial recipients of philosophy, including their own. We have already briefly discussed the difference between 'theory' and 'practice'. Moral philosophy can afford to eliminate *phronesis*, yet practice cannot. Without getting practice in *phronesis* philosophers will carry their absolutes into their daily practice, and then only good luck will rescue them from becoming well-meaning pawns in the service of evil powers (Sartre, for example, had good luck). When Foucault became involved in movements for prison reform, he must have been aware of the fact that this practice did not follow from his philosophy; he did it all the same, because it was the right thing to do. One can also speak about the living, for example, Habermas, who has never spared himself from being involved in practical matters of formidable moral and political importance. The philosopher can be right and wrong as everyone else in action or debate: this is precisely what is exemplary. For it is not the '*philosophe engagé*', but the engaged person who happens also to be a philosopher we are talking about. A *philosophe engagé* is always right (as a philosopher), since he has made everything sound 'right' in the framework of his philosophy, and thus he goes on to realize his 'truth', whereas a philosopher who is an engaged person listens to the judgement of others, considers the situation, the time and the place and is aware of his or her dual responsibility. As a philosopher she or he will remain absolutist (in the framework of philosophy, relativism is just another absolutist stance), but as a person and citizen she or he will learn how to absorb another person's point of view and how to do justice to their life experiences. The universalists will consider everyday intuitions and they will practise their *phronesis*; the advocates of everyday intuitions will appreciate the institutions of liberal democracy, they will practise civic virtues and they will also make a commitment to at least one universal value; and, lastly, the faintly sceptical mouthpieces of the institutions of liberal democracy will appreciate both traditional moral intuitions and universalistic claims. Yet back at their writing desks they will continue to make everything right in one particular way, and will expose all the other paradigms to scorn or to derision. This is neither right nor wrong, but the only thing to do in the dense medium of philosophical speculation.

There is only one concrete *moral* rule of the game that should be heeded, and I mention it for the last time: as long as a philosopher has not done something morally reprehensible, the rejection of the dangerous implications of a philosophy should not extend to the rejection of the person – even labelling the person is strongly unwarranted. Conversely, if the person has done something reprehensible, the moral judgement passed on the person should not be extended to their philosophy as a whole, because theoretical and practical judgements are different in kind. Yet only fundamentalists can deny our right to show the possible connections between a philosophy and a philosopher's morally reprehensible attitude or action. It is mere fundamentalism to restrict the rethinking of one of the oldest philosophical doctrines or convictions. Pre-modern philosophy took it as self-evident that philosophers 'live' their philosophy. Do they still do so? One can answer the question in both ways, but one cannot seriously believe that it is an anti-philosophical gesture to raise this question once again and to try to answer it.

Notes

1 *Zerstorung des moralischen Selbstbewusstseins: Chance oder Gefahrung?* (Frankfurt: Suhrkamp, 1988).
2 Karl-Otto Apel, 'Zurück zur Normalität? Oder könnten wir aus der nationalen Katastrophe etwas Besonderes gelernt haben?' in ibid., pp. 49–66.
3 Otto Poggeler, 'Besinnung oder Ausflucht? Heideggers ursprungliches Denken', in ibid., pp. 238–72.

4 Richard Rorty, 'Der Vorrang der Demokartie vor der Philosophie', in ibid., pp. 273–90.

5 G. W. F. Hegel, *History of Philosophy*, vols 1 and 2. For example, he writes in the introduction to his discussion on sophism: 'Unsere gelehrte Professoren sind insofern viel unschuldiger als die Sophisten; um diese Unschuldigkeit gibt aber die Philosophie nichts' (*Vorlesungen über die Geschichte der Philosophie*, vol. 1, in *Werke*, vol. 18, Frankfurt: Suhrkamp, 1971). That Hegel saw some justification in the indictment against Socrates and also in his death sentence is a part of Hegel's story, but not of mine.

6 See, in detail, A. Heller, *Radical Philosophy* (Oxford: Blackwell, 1984).

6

The Concept of the
Political Revisited

I

In giving the title *The Concept of the Political* to his *opus magnum* on political philosophy,[1] Carl Schmitt coined a term that was representative of a trend emerging during and after the First World War, for a radical opposition to mainstream political philosophies of the second part of the nineteenth century had surfaced in the war-torn countries. The traditions that were thus dismissed ranged from liberalism to the Marxism of the Second International. They stood accused of weakness and inadequate imagination, pathetic incompetence and philosophical impotence. Political imagination, so the post-war commentators believed, could be restored to its former power and dignity by an authentic political philsophy that presented, or rather discovered, the sole and all-embracing concept of the political. This concept should point out the very quality (or factor) that, if generally inherent, transforms 'every thing' from a 'mere thing' into a 'political thing'. There could be only a single quality or factor (for example, a relation, an act or something else) the presence or absence of which determines whether or not a relation, an action, a conflict is political in nature.

There are two theoretical alternatives for grounding a philosophical concept of the political. First, 'the political' can be seen as 'a certain thing' (a quality, a factor) that other 'things' can share as well as not. Second, 'the political' can also be conceived of as a domain, for example a sphere or a system. Whatever enters this domain becomes political in nature when it enters; whatever exits from this domain ceases to be political when it makes its exit.

The 'concept of the political' as a philosophical device was unknown in pre-modern thought. Even cultures with the strongest political awareness, for example the Greek and the Roman, shared the quasi-naturalistic, and therefore unproblematic, view that only acts that have been decided upon and done by the members of the political class(es) can be termed political. When members of a political class, whether a caste, an estate or something else, act in their capacity as members of this class, their acts are, by definition, political. The acts of all others are, whatever their concrete character, non-political. Slaves cannot engage in politics, nor can women, unless they are very highly placed in the hierarchy of the political class. Institutions established and run by the members of political classes are political; other institutions are non-political.

This simple equation of the 'political quality' with the acts of the members of political classes accounts for the transparency of pre-modern political institutions. In this setting, political categories can be coined in a direct and non-reified manner. The question then is not *what* but *who* the state is. In Aristotle's formulation, the state is just the sum total of its citizens; in that of Louis XIV: 'L'état c'est moi.'

Modernity changes all this, slowly at first, later with ever-increasing speed. Liberalism and modern democracy do not speak the language of a political class as a natural tongue, despite the powerful efforts of early liberals and democrats to create a political class once again. In this, as in so many other cases, the language is revealing. As Marx, and later Weber, noticed, modernity did produce a political bureaucracy but definitely no new political class proper. The birth of modern mass democracy finally discarded the equation of political class with political action. It was at this historical juncture that the question concerning the character of 'the political' could appear on the agenda; a criterion had to be found for determining which actions, phenomena and institutions are of political provenance and which are not.

Similar problems arise if the closely related issue, that of institutions, is addressed. In modern times, the question of 'who the state is' does not make much sense; one should rather ask *what* it is. Most theorists know quite well that the state, just as all other political institutions, consists of a network of human relations. But modern institutions, including the political institutions, manifest a kind of internal logic and learning capacity by virtue of which they can be described as systems. The use of reified categories is necessary for understanding them. Philosophy, for its part, cannot operate with reified categories; the language game called philosophy simply does not allow for this kind of procedure. Put briefly, the opacity of appearances is an obstacle for the philosophical gambit.

The increasing complexity of appearances in the political network of modernity had already been noticed by Kant and Hegel. Yet they made no attempt to coin a 'concept of the political'. This fact, among others, accounts for the rejection of, or disregard for, their respective political philosophies by the positivist/utilitarian mainstream and the emergent new philosophical radicalism. The political philosophies of Kant and Hegel were discovered when the ambiguities, and in certain cases the dangerous connotations, of the celebrated 'concept of the political' appeared in full relief, following the Second World War.

II

The concept of the political yields radical political philosophies. Not every radical philosophy is also a radical *political* philosophy, nor is every radical political philosophy accompanied by political radicalism. Yet, the strong affinity of the concept of the political with political radicalism at both extremes of the political spectrum is part and parcel of our story.

It was perhaps Max Weber who made the first opening towards the concept of the political.[2] After him, 'the concept of the political' was immediately divorced from sociology, and embarked upon its exclusively philosophical career.

Carl Schmitt, the godfather of the concept of the political, lent the elegant form of a succinct political philosophy to his own action theory. Although the supreme political act is the act of decision,[3] Schmitt contended, the concept of the political is not sovereignty but the binary 'friend and foe'.[4] Politics is tantamount to fighting for and against someone, not for and against something. 'Friend and foe' are the categories of value-orientation in politics, just as are 'beautiful and ugly' in aesthetics or 'good and evil' in morals. Politics is direct action, mass action, in which friends are mobilized against foes. Schmitt's concept of 'the political' is thus tantamount to a permanent state of war against both external and internal enemies. Here, acting is juxtaposed to talking, struggling to compromise, discord to concord, and so on. His book too is a political act, direct action of a kind in so far as its primary aim is to destroy liberalism, the despicable enemy of political radicalism.

Even if we disregard the well-known political connotations of the thesis (which did not escape the attention of Ortega y Gasset, already at that time one of the leading Spanish liberals[5]), the succinctness and elegance of Schmitt's formula hardly compensates for the loss of whole, important dimensions of political life in his vision of the political. Several political institutions have absolutely nothing to do with the distinction between 'friend and foe'. This is why, in Schmitt's conception, the value of the political is not inherent in them and why they are dismissed from the domain of the political. In this vision, actions undertaken on behalf of something and not at the same time against someone are, by definition, unpolitical; so are speech acts aiming at mutual understanding. My main objection to Schmitt's version of the concept of the political is not that it is one-sided, a common feature of all innovative philosophical ideas, but that it acquires its philosophical thrust from exclusion. It is therefore more than radical; it is a thoroughly tyrannical formulation of the concept of the political.

The same objection cannot be made against the representative versions of existentialist radicalism in political philosophy, for example those of Lukács and Heidegger. Two brief remarks will suffice by way of introduction. First, I restrict the discussion of Lukács to the years between 1921 and 1923[6] and that of Heidegger to those between 1933 and 1934.[7] My reason is that only their respective political philosophies conceived in these periods can be termed 'existential'. I will not take issue here with their respective political affiliations. Second, in what follows, I will restrict my analysis to their concepts of the political.

Like Weber, both Lukács and Heidegger embrace the Kierkegaardian paradox of the existential choice. But, unlike Weber, they transpose the choice from the individual to a collectivity. In Kierkegaard, much as in Weber, it is the person who can choose himself existentially. He chooses absolutely what he is and thus his destiny in becoming what he is. Modern individuals for the most part are aware of their ontological contingency. It therefore makes perfect sense that contingent persons destine themselves by choosing themselves absolutely. If an existential choice comes off, the person becomes as free as an individual can be. For everything persons now do will follow from their character, which is tantamount to their chosen destiny.

Lukács and Heidegger, as young radicals, had several features in common. They both made a bid for the intersubjective constitution of the world; they both rejected their own age as petty and banausic, as a world devoid of greatness, heroism, tragedy and destiny. The idea of a *collective* existential choice thus emerged almost naturally in their closely similar vision and theoretical interest. The political appeared to them as the identity of the essence and existence of a community. When a collective entity chooses itself and thus its own destiny, the political act *par excellence* has already been accomplished. In Lukács it is the empirical proletariat, this merely economic class, that is bound to choose itself and thus its own destiny. The moment of the proletarian revolution is the very moment of constituting the political. In Heidegger, it is the nation, the empirical German nation, that is bound to become fully political in the gesture of self-choice. This is what happens in the 'German revolution', which is a political gesture *par excellence*. On the purely theoretical plane, the philosophy of existential choice does not exclude Others. Lukács recasts the Marxian dictum that the proletariat cannot liberate itself without liberating the whole of humankind in the vision of a final redemption. For Heidegger, Germany had just set a general example. For all nations of the world can choose themselves existentially, and, once they do, they can live together in perpetual peace.

There is no need to illustrate the degree to which the radical philosophy of this time was out of tune with practice. This aside, there are good theoretical grounds for thinking that the paradigm of collective consciousness (or collective *Dasein*) authorizes the repression of individual conscience and freedom. The concept of a collective existential choice is mythological, because it conceives of a modern collectivity, for example a class or a nation, in terms of an individual, a single person of gigantic dimensions, formidable powers and unitary will. In these philosophies, the world is transposed into a new Olympus where heroic dramas are acted out. If carried out completely, this conceptual operation results in the total loss of the perception of reality.

The theoretical flaw of the philosophy of collective existential choice is inseparable from its political implications. The self-choice of a collectivity, if possible at all, cannot be existential. The collective entity is not an 'exister', to use Kierkegaard's term; thus it cannot choose its existence. Individuals can indeed choose themselves because they, and they alone, are 'existers'. In choosing themselves they can become free. A collective existential choice could not make persons, real individuals, free. Since not every worker or every German would choose himself or herself existentially, even less would all of them choose themselves as persons committed to the party (the alleged carrier of collective destiny), the philosophy of collective existential choice cannot help but legitimize the oppression of individuals. It deserves a brief mention here that, although both Lukács and Heidegger very quickly abandoned their self-created mythological devices, the existential concept of the political had its comeback in Sartre's thesis of the 'project' and in his theory of the radicalization of Evil.

Hannah Arendt was the only representative philosopher with a life-long attachment to the concept of the political who was never committed to the extremes of political radicalism. On the contrary. Her book on totalitarianism may perhaps be considered the philo-sophically most eloquent statement on, and condemnation of, radical extremism and its consequences.[8] Arendt in fact shared Ortega's concern that the demise of the ancient political classes can leave a void to be occupied by the mob. Rendering politics not only banausic but also banal was Arendt's major concern. It is at this point that her vision relates to that of political radicalism. Arendt's favourite dream was the emergence, or re-emergence, of a democratic political class. Such a political class would be constituted by active citizens, men and women who are permanently committed to political action, who devote their lives to sitting in council with their fellow-citizens in order to discuss matters of state. It was the exalted idea of ancient citizenship that inspired Arendt's mind.

In Arendt's theory, the concept of the political is action as *energeia*.[9] The category *energeia* includes direct action, discussion and theoretical activity. Therefore it should by no means be associated with *action directe*. Action is the act that is an end in itself. If practised in the public domain, such action is, by definition, political; in fact, it is 'the political'. This is why early American townships and Hungarian workers' councils alike appealed to Arendt. For her, as for almost all other advocates of the concept of the political, the greatest moment of 'the political' is revolution. With her uncompromising hostility to both mob politics and hero worship *and* with her life-long commitment to the democratic legacy, she stands out as a solitary great figure among the protagonists of modern radical political philosophy. And yet she shares many of their basic tenets, sometimes even their visions. Her emphasis on new beginning and its recurrence, her strong distinction between political activism and mere passive citizenship, her longing for the restoration of a political class, together with her contemptuous treatment of merely social issues, or even of the 'social question' as such, all this belonged to the arsenal of political radicalism.

It comes as no surprise, then, that Arendt was, despite the sophistication of her theory, occasionally exposed to the malaise that, as a rule, accompanies the concept of the political: the fury of exclusion. Human groups or diverging opinions are, of course, not excluded from her theory; but issues are. In fact, far too many issues have to be excluded from the concept of the political, if we are to accept her understanding of the concept. Again, it is not the resolute one-sidedness of Arendt's political vision that I question here; rather, I take issue with her self-created dilemma, namely being committed to democracy while at the same time excluding a wide variety of issues that men and women perceive as political affairs of the greatest urgency in their daily lives. This obsession with the exclusively political, as well as the disregard for 'mere daily practices', is a typical problematic feature of the radical branch of political philosophy.

If my critical comments are correct, the question should inevitably be posed whether political *philosophy* has any more options left. Or rather, the very moment that one loses the feeling of having been party to a mythological adventure, one also leaves the domain of political philosophy proper and enters into the sober atmosphere of sociology or political science. The controversy surrounding the concept of the political is more than just another family quarrel among paradigms; it is about the relevance or irrelevance of political philosophy to our times. The concept of the political came to the rescue of political philosophy after it had fallen victim to too much science, too much compromise, too much realism. Should we aim at the restoration of the *status quo ante* with regard to the concept of the political, or are there other avenues still to explore?

III

The final and dialectical unity of normative claims and empirical awareness is the absolute precondition of the possibility of political philosophy. Viewed from this angle, political philosophy has realized itself in modernity, or, in other words, modernity is the age when political philosophy came to pass. Philosophy has never stopped insisting that what is regarded as truth is not really the truth, but that something else is true, or that what is regarded to be just is not just, because something else would be more, or even perfectly, just. The more we reflect upon the structure of modernity and its *modus operandi*, the more it reminds us of philosophy. The very essence of the modern condition comprises the contradiction between Is and Ought as well as their – always only momentary – sublation. The famous dictum that all men are born free but are everywhere in chains is an extreme but apposite and concise summary of the situation. Modernity is a turning point in histories, in so far as it is here and now that universal values become politically effective. What hitherto has happened only in philosophy can and does now happen in political practice and life. Men and women constantly juxtapose Ought, that is, universalized values, to Is, to their political and social institutions, which fail to match or live up to Ought. Men and women interpret and reinterpret those values in their daily practices and they go about using them as vehicles of critique and refutation, of realizing philosophy or philosophy's ultimate end.[10]

The modern concept of the political – or, to avoid tautology, the concept of the political as such – is to be derived from the quintessence of modern political dynamic. In actual fact, this is precisely what all radical political philosophers have always done, and yet they have all ended up excluding large territories of the political from the concept of the political. Worse still, many of them ended up excluding 'the others', that is, whole human groups from the political domain. This was the result of supplying a substantive political definition for the concept of the political. We thus face the following dilemma. If no substantive definition is given to the concept of the political, the concept itself vanishes – at least, the political character of the very relation, value, network, choice, act or anything else under discussion has to be defined in order to forge such a concept. If, however, the substantive definition is of political provenance (for example, the collective existential choice or the dichotomy of friend and foe), we are back at our initial predicament: exclusion.

What have been the results of this enquiry so far? The political philosophy of an epoch without political classes, one of increasing complexity and increasing opacity, needs a concept of the political. This concept has to be substantively, but not strongly, defined. However, the substantive definition must not be political in nature. What kind of definition can this possibly be?

I have already set a few limits to this search. The concept we are looking for must be an authentic concept of the political. Either it must indicate what the thing is that, if added to others, makes them 'political', and/or it must pinpoint the domain in which 'any thing' that enters it will be transformed into a political thing. The concept needs to contain and make manifest the tension between Ought and Is in its existence and *modus operandi* in modern societies. For example, if the substantive content given to the political is ethical in character, this ethical content cannot be merely normative nor can it be merely empirical. This is why the categorical imperative as such does not qualify for the concept of the political. On the other hand, defining the concept of the political in terms of 'a routine of cheating and lying' or as 'mere manipulation' is meaningless because it disregards the existence of rules of the game without which the terms 'cheating' or 'bending the rules' are empty. If politics is indeed a kind of cheating, the norms or rules political actors employ to cheat and manipulate also belong to the 'ethical substance' of politics, if there is any.

To grasp the tension between Is and Ought is a general stipulation, but the concept of the political has an additional requirement. 'Is' and 'Ought', as they are contained and made manifest by the concept, must be of a kind that is central for the operation and the dynamic of modern societies. Thus, if the concept of the political has ethical constituents, they must perforce be central to the political life of modernity, and the political actors must be aware of their centrality.

A short list of Oughts that are effective in modern politics can be easily drawn up. Of them, freedom is the most significant. As a completely universalized value, it is open to a great variety of interpretations. In our discourse we operate with many kinds of negative and positive freedoms, such as civic liberties, lack of economic restraints, national independence, personal and institutional autonomy, and the like. Freedom can be effectively used as an 'ought term' in all its interpretations whenever actors apply them as regulative or constitutive practical ideas. In addition to freedom and its interpretations, many other normative terms are lavishly used by political actors, such as equality, the value of 'life', decent life. Values, such as freedom, equality, peace, rationality and several others, exist as politically effective concepts because they are powerful both as imaginary institutions and in their institutionalized forms as rights.

Universal, quasi-universal and other politically effective values are initially abstract, in the Hegelian sense of the word. They are concretized in a series of conflicts, in contestations about their definitions. When two interpretations of the same value cannot be institutionalized simultaneously, or the interpretations of two values are on a collision course, one carries victory over another in conflicts. Yet, once the basic freedoms have been institutionalized, no such victory can be final. The 'field' is constantly filled with more and more definitions and this is how the politically effective values are, in different ways, made concrete. The process can be conceived of as never-ending, at least pragmatically (for in human life and society everything is finite), although tradition makes certain further practical definitions of freedom more likely than others. Hegel's 'end of history' can very easily be interpreted in this spirit.

Modern society is a complex of conflicting developmental tendencies. For discussion here I have selected three independent logics on a collision course or in a state of coexistence and cooperation.[11] The first is the development of modern technology. The second is the functionality of the social division of labour, by which I mean a social arrangement in terms of which it is not the social division of labour as a quasi-natural type of stratification that defines the functions people are supposed to perform in society, but rather the functions they actually perform that finally stratify them. The third is the practice of statescraft with a view to universalized or quasi-universalized and effective values. In Western modernity these three logics have been concretized in the form of industrialization, competitive market society (capitalism) and liberal democracy. The general redefinition of the first logic is now taking place, while the redefinition of the second is in the making in certain areas (for example, in Scandinavia). All three logics are future-oriented. The first logic cannot be considered as the process of concretization of the major modern universal, freedom, because it produces the conditions for both unfreedom and freedom. The third logic spearheads the threefold process in several aspects. Certain state institutions are devised as the main carriers or guarantees of the effective universal values in more than one of its interpretations. The rights of man and citizen are a case in point here, as are representative government and the division of powers. Modern representative government is the first kind of governance that opens up the avenue to overcoming patriarchy. Hitherto, direct democracy has always remained the patriarchy of equal brothers. There is no independent political person without mediation: and without the powerful idea of an independent political person, which is yet another interpretation of the value of freedom, organic entities remain the ultimate political units. Mediation is more than a mere catchword, for it grasps one of the main determinations of the modern concept of the political.

Freedom, as well as other values, becomes effective not only through the unfolding of the third logic of modernity, but through the unfolding of the second logic as well. The separation of the organic–genetic and the social determinations of human life is the ontological source of both positive and negative freedom. Men and women are now being reduced to a bundle of undetermined and – in principle –

also unlimited possibilities. It is thus that they are set free. Yet the conditions for the actual use of freedom are absent in several aspects. The functionality of the social division of labour drives people towards greater competitiveness, but not towards the readiness for a manifold interpretation and concretization of the politically effective values. However, universal or quasi-universal imaginary institutions can serve as the frame of reference for all kinds of contestation. Men and women can thus politicize all issues that affect the conditions of the use of their potential freedoms in non-political institutions as well as in daily life. Put briefly, the concretization of the universal values and other main effective political values proceeds in modern societies at several levels, directly or indirectly, provided that there exists a public space to ensure and to secure the contestation itself. The very existence of a public space and the right to use it, a right open to everyone after the demise of the political class(es), guarantees the choice between using and not using it. The actors themselves decide whether or not a particular issue should be brought into the public space.

In actual fact, men and women frequently concretize one or another universal or quasi-universal value without politicizing the issue. This happens particularly when it is the value of 'rationality' that needs to be further concretized. It happens quite rarely that the rationalization of institutions becomes a matter of public concern, unless other values are also involved in the process of contestation. It usually happens on such occasions that we refer to so-called 'mere' technical problems. In those modern societies that have neither rights nor a public space, it becomes quite impossible to separate political from non-political contestations. This is why all issues related to values of any kind become thoroughly politicized both by those who rule and by those who are ruled.

IV

The concretization of the universal value of freedom in the public domain is the modern concept of the political.

The concept defines the domain of 'the political'. Whatever enters this field becomes political; whatever exits from it ceases to be political. The concrete character of things that enter or exit has been left undefined. In fact, everything that satisfies some other criteria of the 'political' becomes actually political if men and women so decide that it should be discussed, contested, decided in the public domain;

similarly, something can cease to be political if they take it off the agenda of public concerns.

Within the 'domain' of the political, that is the public space, things can become 'political' to a greater or lesser extent through actions, institutions, opinions, discussions, propositions, goals, and the like, depending upon their 'share' in 'the political'. The substantive aspect of 'the political' is not a concrete political 'thing' at all; rather, it is the main dynamism of modernity itself. No action of a concrete structure, no momentous choice, no particular orientative value specific to politics alone is the criterion or the standard of 'the political'.

The concretization of freedom can take place in the form of struggle between friend and foe, as well as in that of concerted cooperation and discussion, and in several other ways and forms. A great amount of political 'substance' of this kind may be inherent in men and women choosing politics as a vocation as well as in those who enter the public space for only a brief moment but make an exceptionally strong impact there. No one and nothing is excluded in principle. The contrast of Ought and Is, as well as their sublation, inheres in this concept of the political. The concept is both normative and empirical. It can equally well be interpreted in a near-redemptive, progressivist, sceptical or positively nihilistic scenario. The near-redemptive paradigm may give voice to the hope that Ought and Is will finally coalesce. The progressivist scenario may vest its optimism in the likelihood of a further and uninhibited concretization of the universal value of freedom through dialogue, compromise and cooperation. The sceptical version may envision the modern world as the battlefield of conflicting and contradictory concretizations of this value, where one concretization will be erased and replaced by another. The nihilistic scenario may project on to the screen of the future the image of self-destruction by freedom. And yet they could all subscribe to the concept of the political that has been proposed here. This concept is modern in the sense that it is accompanied by different visions of history.

Why is the modern concept of the political tantamount to the concretization of freedom? Why is it not equivalent to, or coextensive with, the concretization of other eminent values of modernity, such as rationality, equality or peace?

Rationality, equality and peace, and many other values besides, belong to the arsenal of the politically active values, if, and only if, their concretization is directly or indirectly connected with the cause of freedom (for example, directly in the case of 'equal rights', indirectly in the case of 'equal salary for equal work'). Regardless of whether 'perpetual peace in philosophy', as Kant envisioned it, is desirable or undesirable, it is certainly not a political issue.

It is not written in the stars whether or not a particular cause is related to the issue of freedom; it can be closely related to it on one occasion and severed from it in another. Men and women, citizens, political agents, may or may not interpret an attempt to concretize a certain value as an issue of their freedom or that of the freedom of others. This is how they politicize and depoliticize issues, sometimes the very same ones.

This restriction also applies to the public domain. There are institutions constantly and directly related to freedom in this domain, such as the government, the press, the institutions and procedures of legislation, and so on. Actually, all issues upon which decisions, in full or in part, are made by political institutions can be 'politicized' without difficulty. However, if the issue has no connection with freedom in the public eye, one discusses 'policies' and not 'politics' in order to indicate the difference. The public character of an issue does not necessarily make it political, except in a state of tyranny. Similarly, the concretization of freedom alone does not politicize an issue except in a fully totalitarian society.

I defined the concept of the political in the modern world as 'the concretization of the universal value of freedom in the public domain'. I also elucidated, if only briefly, why this concept as a theoretical idea is superior to all others. Here I would add that it is also superior as a practical idea.

As a theoretical idea, the concept of the political can be associated with four different visions of the world (the near-redemptive, the progressivist, the sceptical and the nihilistic). As a practical idea, it is associated with the commitment to the concretization of the value of freedom. This is because neither the redemptive nor the nihilistic version makes recommendations for proper praxis. As a theoretical idea the concept is void of moral quality; as a practical idea it carries such a content, for the very same reason. On the theoretical plane, the concept of the political does not exclude anything or anyone, and it is thus that it avoids the pitfall of radical political philosophies. On the ethical plane, however, 'anything' does not go. What ought to result from the concretization of freedom – if something ought to result from it at all – is equal freedom of all. The process of the concretization of freedom cannot (should not) thwart the fulfilment of this Ought, irrespective of whether or not one anticipates this happening. Such a commitment is rooted in an *ethos*, which is not as strong as the

Hegelian *Sittlichkeit* but remains an ethos all the same, albeit a weak one. A weak ethos cannot determine what one should do; rather, it consists of shared taboos. Those who accept the modern concept of the political as the regulative idea of political acts certainly impose taboos on racism, or on support lent to blatantly unjust wars, not to mention on genocidal or totalitarian regimes. They also impose taboos on the deliberate exclusion of certain human groups from the public sphere, self-righteous paternalism and much else. A weak ethos also excludes certain goals from the arsenal of our goals, certain judgements and standpoints from the arsenal of our judgements and standpoints, certain pragmatically viable, even useful, options from the arsenal of our options. This is how the modern concept of the political (the concretization of the value of freedom in the public domain) mediates between what 'is' and what 'ought to be'.

Nearing the end of my journey, the goal of which was to retrieve the concept of the political, I must confess that I have not charted unknown territory. Two great explorers embarked on the same trip a long time ago: Kant and Hegel were the first to set foot firmly on the land of modernity, and it is to them that I owe the foundation of the theoretical exploits presented in this essay. However, I have to repeat what has already been stated: neither Kant nor Hegel elaborated a concept of the political.

To recycle fundamental attitudes or even tenets of the Kantian or Hegelian philosophy is not an act of repetition. A recycled dress is a different garment from what has been recycled. Not only does the historical experience of almost two centuries inspire the act of recycling, so do the insights and innovations of radical political philosophers of this century. They were the ones who tied the concept of the political to revolution. The 'concretization of freedom' is also a revolution – not a revolution that 'breaks out' or 'happens', but one that 'takes place'. When it takes place in the public domain, it is political in nature; when it takes place in other domains, then it is not political, yet revolution it certainly remains, for our whole way of life is entirely changed in the process.

Radical political philosophies of this century mythologized politics and juxtaposed political action and choice to the allegedly banal concerns of daily life. The concept of the political that has been suggested here links politics with the daily life of men and women. Modern political philosophy need not be a dithyramb about the Great Event writ large nor a choreography of exceptional political movements. Although politics can be pleasing or displeasing, modern political actors and thinkers should not, in cases of conflict, give preference to aesthetic values, such as elegance, sublimity or perfection, over freedom. It is time to say bid farewell to the legacy of our aristocratic ancestors.

Notes

1 Carl Schmitt, *The Concept of the Political* (New Brunswick, NJ: Rutgers University Press, 1976).
2 Max Weber, 'Politics as a vocation', in Gerth and Mills' collection of Weber's writings (Philadelphia, Fortress Press, 1956).
3 Carl Schmitt, *Political Theology* (Cambridge, Mass.: MIT Press, 1985).
4 Schmitt, *The Concept.*
5 Jose Ortega y Gasset, *Revolt of the Masses* (New York: Norton, 1964).
6 Georg Lukács, *History and Class Consciousness* (Cambridge, Mass.: MIT Press, 1971).
7 Martin Heidegger, *Textes politiques 1933–34. Le Debat* (Paris: Gallimard, ,January/February 1988).
8 Hannah Arendt, *The Origins of Totalitarianism* (New York: Harcourt Brace Jovanovich, 1979).
9 Hannah Arendt, *The Human Condition* (Chicago: University of Chicago Press, 1970).
10 Agnes Heller, *Beyond Justice* (Oxford: Blackwell, 1987).
11 Agnes Heller, *A Theory of History* (London, Routledge & Kegan Paul, 1982). There I differentiated between two logics of civil society and the logic of technological development.

7
Freedom and Happiness in Kant's Political Philosophy

I

Like de Tocqueville who alerted people concerned with public matters to the tension between freedom and equality, Kant predicted the collision between freedom and happiness a few decades earlier. But unlike de Tocqueville, Kant made no efforts to explore the possible results of the conflict. Rather, he aspired to establish normatively the unconditional priority of freedom over happiness throughout his whole theoretical system. Kants' rule has been more recently baptized by Rawls the 'priority rule'.[1] However, it is not the Rawlsian version but rather the pristine Kantian form of the theory that will be at the centrepoint of the following meditations.

Kant's greatness, like the greatness of philosophies in general, lies in the simplicity of the fundamental innovations on which his systematic edifice rests: the division of the Subject into two uninterrelated subjects, as well as the celebrated 'Copernican revolution'.[2] In actual fact, the two innovations were but one. Without the division of the subject into two uninterrelated subjects, the critique of pure reason could not have been accomplished; without the Copernican revolution, the divided subject would have remained a more streamlined version of the old distinction between *res cogitans* and *res extensa*. The unavoidable dogmatism hidden behind the Kantian concept of Freedom, i.e. Will, i.e. Pure Practical Reason, which has been pointed out many times, is irrelevant once we address the problem of the *modus operandi* of the Kantian innovation. The moment we accept the gambit and take it for granted that every human being simultaneously resides in two completely different worlds, one of Freedom and one of Nature, sharing the first with all intelligible beings and the second with all inorganic and organic beings, all the problems of practical philosophy that the men of enlightenment struggled with become pseudo-problems. With one gesture they are all solved. Kant insisted in his 'Speculative Beginning of Human History'[3] that there is only a seeming contradiction between the two groups of Rousseau's *oeuvre*, even if the author was unaware both of the contradiction and of its merely apparent nature. For in the first group of his works Rousseau discusses the human race as 'nature' and in the second the human race as 'moral', that is, as free. The only remaining question is whether or not one accepts the gambit.

Dividing every individual subject into a sensible creature and a super-sensible creature opened up a virtually inexhaustible field of vision for Kant and for all succeeding generations who still bother to read him. The psychological problem of whether Kant was devising a theoretical system in order to pose, and at the same time philosophically solve, all the questions to which he already knew the answers, or whether unforeseen and surprisingly novel issues were born out of the new approach itself, deserves thought, but it cannot be addressed here. The problem in reverse is our main topic. Can one subscribe to certain main conclusions of the Kantian practical philosophy in general, and the Kantian political philosophy in particular, without a commitment to the philosophy of the divided subject? More concretely: can the principle of the absolute priority of freedom over happiness be maintained, and, if so, can it be maintained to the extent and in the fashion Kant wanted it, without accepting the schism of our race into a rational and a sensual half, thereby splitting ourselves into freedom and nature?

II

Kant relegates happiness to the background of his moral philosophy.[4] In contrast to the venerable philosophical tradition from Aristotle to Spinoza and even further, he does not list virtuousness or righteousness among the main sources of happiness. The upright man is worthy of happiness, but whether he is happy or not is merely an empirical question. Kant, for his part, seems to believe that he is not. At first glance, this contention transpires as some kind of realistic description; but much more is at stake here. For whether moral goodness is a source of happiness is as little a merely empirical question as, for example, the issue of whether reason is the source of moral goodness. The question of what happiness really is needs to be decided first. Whereas Kant's concept of freedom is overrefined, his concept of happiness is almost conventional, with one important twist. Happiness, both for Kant and for the proverbial 'man in the street', consists of satisfying our desires, achieving our goals, succeeding in the pursuit of our interests. The Kantian twist is the philosopher's firm view that chasing happiness is like chasing ghosts. Driven by their three most forceful motivations, the hunger for fame, power and wealth, people will never be satiated. The more we crave happiness, the more it eludes us. Regardless of whether or not one is worthy of happiness, one will not be happy in any case. A good person who is worthy of happiness could actually become happy if two conditions were met. First, happiness needs to be possible for worthy and unworthy alike, that is, human desires should, as a rule, be satiable; second, satiable desires should be in perfect harmony with goodness, that is, with acting under the guidance of the moral law.

Goodness is unconditional on two counts: the imperative to be followed is categorical and condition–indifferent (what one ought to do one can do under any condition). The happiness of man, however, in so far as it is possible at all, is conditional throughout. Its first condition is fulfilled by nature owing to human action, but without human design. With a dialectic twist, it is the insatiable character of our needs as the manifestation of the advancement of culture that is seen as the major step towards the fulfilment of the first condition. The second condition is freedom, this time not internal (moral) but external (legal). As long as needs develop faster than freedom expands, we continue to live in a state of war and unhappiness. Political philosophy is practical philosophy that sets as its task the formulation of principles under whose guidance the signs can be reversed. Political philosophy asks the question: how should we act such that freedom expands faster than needs increase or at least such that it should not lag behind?

The state in which the expansion of freedom does not lag behind the increase of needs is termed by Kant the republic; the age of the republic is termed the enlightened age.[5] Kant never ceases to emphasize that his own – modern – age is not an enlightened one but one of enlightenment; not the age of the republic, but a transitory period in which the basic pillars of a republic should be erected. Such a republic could in turn lead to the unity of freedom and nature in a very distant future. This forceful idea, which compromises the ultimate end of history as nature, cannot be lost from sight, because it alone can give sense and meaning to our acts from a political (albeit not moral) point of view. This is the historical, as well as the near-soteriological, setting in which the modern political conflict between freedom and happiness is acted out on the stage of Kant's philosophy.

Kant derives the three principles of the republican constitution from practical reason, that is from Freedom.[6] In Kant's view, it would have been completely impossible to derive them from empirical observation, for two reasons: first, no extant institution embodies those principles; second, empirical persons in empirical situations can never establish them.

Kant thus divorces the immense political power of future-oriented ideas in modern life, and the centrality of the idea of freedom among them. He also wants to secure the 'lawful' use of this tremendous power of collective imagination. To that end he needs to specify the lawful interpretation of Freedom. To derive the three principles of a free political state from Freedom, that is, from pure practical reason, is certainly the only theoretically consistent way of doing so that is at the same time politically safe. But, then, nothing that Kant attributes to man's nature (and not to his freedom), such as feelings, desires, interest or goals of any kind, can participate in the discovery of the principles of freedom and in maintaining them against overwhelming odds. Kant's well-known reference to the French Revolution in his late work *The Conflict of the Faculties*[7] sounds exaggerated and perplexing if one loses sight of his emphatic stricture on transcensus. That the enthusiastic involvement of the spectators in the idea of freedom could be appraised by Kant as the guarantee of a future unification of nature and freedom sounds odd (particularly for us, who witness this phenomenon almost every day, and sometimes with little sympathy), unless we remember that in Kant's universe no feeling should have anything to do with ideas, particularly not with the idea of Freedom.

The second stipulation concerns the act of foundation. Kant learned his Rousseau well: if the founding act results from the will of all, no free constitution will come about. Empirical persons have different ends and concepts of happiness, so their (empirical) wills must collide. And when they are after the same end, the result is even worse, namely a conflict of interests. Kant also agrees with Rousseau on the point that men can be free only if they obey self-imposed laws, but he cannot go along with the Rousseauian concept of the General Will. If the will-to-freedom does not reside in every individual, the act of foundation miscarries, resulting in despotism. Actually, there is only one philosophical solution of the problem: the will-to-freedom that dwells in all of us should be identical. Since it cannot be identical in content, it must be identical in form. It is thus that we return to Freedom, that is, pure practical reason (rational humankind that dwells in all of us) as the only legitimate legislator. The stage is now re-set: all men legislate, and equally so, not in their capacity as concrete individuals, but in their capacity as specimens of the collective and universal subject called rational humankind.

The three principles of freedom on which every republic is forever based are the following: the freedom of all men[8] as members of society, the equality of persons as subjects, and the independence of every member of the commonwealth as a burgher. In the first principle, Kant makes a case for the negative (liberal) concept of freedom, in the third for the positive, democratic concept of freedom (every member of the political body participates in legislation), and in the second for freedom as equality before the law, that is, for liberties as rights. This is a comprehensive list of the modern interpretations of political freedom. All three principles are foundational. They do not comprise a constitution; rather the constitutions of all republics should be founded on them irrespective of their differences. To use contemporary jargon: the three principles, and nothing else, are required as the background consensus to establish a republic. Concrete republican institutions can change, yet the principles of freedom are eternal. By using the term 'eternal' Kant did not mean to imply that the principles of freedom derive from divine ordinance, but rather that they follow from reason. The laws of reason are eternal since they are not subjected to change.

Kant never ceases to emphasize that a good constitution (even the best) has nothing to do with the happiness of the people who live under this constitution. Furthermore, he insists that happiness, or the issue of happiness, has no positive relation to politics at all. Politics (and law) is about freedom, not about happiness. Whenever he pinpoints a connection between them, it is invariably negative. The desire for happiness makes us unfree, the pursuit of happiness destroys even the hope of entering the enlightened age of republican constitutions. *Salus rei publicae*, so Kant argues in his *Metaphysics of Morals*,[9] has nothing to do with happiness. Perhaps Rousseau was right, Kant ruminates; the primitives were invariably happier than we.

One should not draw from all of this the conclusion that Kant remained indifferent to other people's suffering or happiness. As a moral being, one should care for the happiness of other human beings. Yet to promote another person's happiness is a conditional duty, whereas we are unconditionally duty bound to respect and to honour another person's freedom and rights. It remains to be seen whether the same, or a similar, distinction, this time between conditional and unconditional principles rather than duties, makes sense on the political plane for Kant as well as for ourselves. The 'priority rule' is, at any rate, more manifest in Kant's doctrine of virtue than in his strictly political writings. This rule applies in cases of conflict between the two kinds of duties, but only in such cases. In addition, priority is not tantamount to exclusivity.

Kant locates happiness in need satisfaction. All needs are rooted in man-as-nature or are co-determined by reason and nature. Pure practical reason produces ends that do not promise satisfaction. In Kant, need satisfaction – more precisely, the orientation towards need satisfaction – keeps us in servitude both internally (that is, as moral beings) and externally (that is, as political beings). Actually, Kant identifies three clusters of needs, but refers only to the second cluster whenever he talks about the political aspect of the conflict between freedom and happiness. This second cluster encompasses culturally created needs, which expand constantly (and faster than freedom). These are never merely 'natural', for they are co-determined by reason, yet they are still embedded in a natural tendency of the human race. Moreover, the expansion of the need structure enhances the original inclination. I have mentioned them already: they are the lust for power, wealth and fame. Later references to them in Marxian terminology as 'alienated need structures' is not unwarranted modernization. On a descriptive level there is no difference between Rousseau and Kant at this point. After all, it was Rousseau who insisted that evil results not from desire but from comparison, which is the product of culture. However, Kant is sympathetic to the development of culture, and closer to Hegel and Marx than to Rousseau on this count: his aim is to find the arrangement within which the expansion of cultural needs becomes politically harmless. The issue that he disregards is that the expansion of certain culturally created needs and the satisfaction of other, equally culturally created, ones could become the very conditions for the practice of freedom. At this point, Kant's concrete political perspectives did not keep pace with his broad modernist philosophical vision. The events of the French Revolution assumed cosmic dimensions for Kant, but they were too exceptional, too much out of pattern, to influence his institutional fantasy. It is here that I see a major flaw in Kant's political philosophy.

The third cluster of needs in Kant's philosophy is a combination of nature and reason to the same extent as the second, the 'alienated' kind. They are, however, devoid of the ambiguity of the latter. They are the needs for the society of other human beings. Contrary to 'unsocial sociability' here we could speak of 'social sociability'. Being together with friends, having good conversations, especially about things of beauty, but also about things of interest, is an elementary need the satisfaction of which enhances human dignity; no one is instrumentalized, and social encounter remains a goal in itself. Needs of this kind do not collide with freedom. Yet, satisfying needs of sociability does not require political space, at least not in Kant's mind. Friendship rather than citizenship is the institution where needs such as these can be satisfied or thwarted. This distinction is sound both empirically and normatively. It accounts for the actual development of modernity, and it erects a barrier against the dangerous overpolitization of social relations. But Hannah Arendt has a point, too, when she shifts the weight of Kant's political philosophy away from the issue of legislation for freedom towards a model of political discourse. Arendt can do this with some ease because she shares Kant's deepest suspicions of happiness, i.e. needs and need satisfaction, as a matter for a political agenda, and as the main motivational force of political action. It would be difficult to maintain that Kant wanted to exclude discussions of need-claims from the public domain, because he made a very strong point to the contrary as early as his celebrated pamphlet 'What is Enlightenment?',[10] insisting that everything that should not be questioned within the framework of private institutions could be a legitimate topic for contestation in public. However, he denied that participation in such an ongoing political discussion could be motivated by anything other than duty. And duty is definitely not a need. This is the second flaw in Kant's view of the relation between freedom and happiness in his political philosophy. (Let me mention in parentheses that Arendt did not share this flaw because she never endorsed the concept of duality of human nature in its Kantian rigidity.)

III

The reasons behind Kant's dismissal of 'happiness' from the political domain are serious and need to be addressed first.

Many of us would reject the Kantian interpretation of happiness as pedestrian. Instead of experiencing the raptures of love, or mystic union, the quiet harmony between us and all those dear to us, we have only to achieve, and, ultimately supersede, specified goals – this is what the Kantian story of happiness is all about. As far as one can be the judge of such matters, Kant as a person seemed to be fairly insensitive towards these subtle kinds of happiness; he always reacted with irritation when they were so much as mentioned. His recurring complaints against nature, which, foolishly, fails to grant as long a life to persons of unique endowments as is necessary for them to achieve everything they are capable of achieving, give vent to feelings that had very deep roots. He could not describe himself as 'happy' not for want of love but for want of the time necessary to know everything and to accomplish at least his system in full. Yet, considering that Goethe's *Faust* interpreted happiness exactly as Kant did, and that it was rather Mephistopheles who tried to lure Faust into hedonistic fancies about 'happiness', we could put less emphasis on Kant's personal character and somewhat more on the 'imaginary institutions of signification' of his times. Needless to say, the interpretation of happiness remains the only decisive common denominator between Kant and Goethe. Goethe never shared Kant's vision of politics, so he can be neither credited with nor criticized for the statements that constitute the centrepoint of Kant's invective against the pursuit of happiness in the political domain.

Let me return to Kant's first principle of political freedom, namely: no one should make (or should be in the position to make) another person happy against their own will. Kant does not ask whether or not someone can be made happy against their will, for the principle is valid regardless of whether the answer is in the affirmative or in the negative. Even if one is able to make another person happy against their will, one should not do so because freedom (autonomy) has priority. This follows from the primacy of practical reason. In fact, Kant believed that people can be made happy against their will. It is the antinomy of practical reason which manifests itself in a historico-political paradox. The paradox reads as follows: as long as people are unfree they can be made happy against their will, precisely because they are unfree. The moment they become free and autonomous, they cannot achieve happiness. Either one is unfree and can be made happy, or one is free and cannot be happy at all. But the paradox did not assume the form of a political dilemma. For Kant there was no dilemma nor was there a choice. Freedom is the only binding law for humans. To choose happiness with unfreedom is not a choice, but a shabby semblance of a choice. To paraphrase Kierkegaard but in the spirit of Kant: once you choose happiness without freedom you actually let others choose for you.

Kant did something here that is of crucial significance: he passed from the personal to the collective subject, from 'I' to 'we'. No one should make, or should be in the position to make, a people happy against its will. Again, Kant did not pose the question whether or not a people can be happy against its own will, he rather stated that none should be. People, just like individual persons, have no choice between freedom and happiness. Should a people choose happiness, it thus re-enters the stage of tutelage, for it lets others choose for itself.

This is the point where Kant dwells at some length on the direct political implications of his philosophy. Tyrants and despots, he says, promise people happiness if only they remain in a state of subservience. Despotism is paternalistic, it provides its subjects with at least the elementary necessities of life. Residing under the protective shield of patronage is comfortable, whereas the way of freedom is strenuous. Although with some hesitation, Kant includes patriarchy in the concept of paternalism. The hesitation is attributable to his times, but Kant's daring gesture is his own. The whole 'fair sex', he insists, should come out from her self-incurred tutelage and learn how to be free.

Kant addresses here our times as much as his own. His argument strikes us with its freshness and its urgency. Totalitarianism still gathers a following with its promise of making people happy by satisfying the elementary needs of all, or even all the needs of all (depending on the ideological context). The moment we start to ponder whether or not tyrants can live up to their promises, whether or not it would be 'reasonable' to sacrifice our freedoms for the satisfaction of certain urgent needs, whether or not we should postpone our bid for freedom until certain needs are satisfied, we wittingly or unwittingly pave the way for tyranny and take servitude upon us. Kant's warning is still valid: whatever the reasons, whatever the consequences, whatever the possibilities, no one under any condition should choose servitude, for this is not a choice. Once can choose only to be free; all concrete choices can be made only afterwards. Similar considerations apply when we encounter the well-known argument that women were happier in the state of dependency than they are now wherever they start their strenuous progress towards freedom. It is irrelevant whether certain women would have indeed remained happier had they stayed under tutelage; since happiness depends on the satisfaction of needs, if one needs servitude one is happier as a slave than as a free person. And yet servitude is not a matter of choice, it is rather the state in which women shirk the task of choosing and let men choose for them. Everything there is to say about happiness should be said, but under the condition of freedom or under the condition of the prior acceptance of the primacy of the principles of freedom.

After all, what can be said about happiness?

Here we turn to the second main argument on behalf of the primacy of freedom over happiness in Kant's political philosophy. Whereas the first can be characterized as the 'priority-of-autonomy' argument, the second can be termed the 'priority-of-universality' argument. Although both arguments are rooted in Kant's dualistic anthropology, there is no *prima facie* reason for us to subscribe to the second simply because we subscribe in full to the first. The substance of the second argument needs to be examined separately.

It was the universality argument and not the autonomy argument that made Kant immune to Rousseau's quandary. Since the law of freedom (the moral law) is universal, and all the ends of empirical men are merely particular, concord ensues from freedom, while discord ensues from the pursuit of happiness. Our unity rests on our pure practical reason alone. Naturally, Kant never ceased to emphasize that impure reason, rather than mere desire, is the most powerful motive behind all unlawful public and private strife. He also hinted at the possibility of using the idea of freedom as a means for the achievement of particular aims, although he never explored the implications of such an eventuality. The conflict is always located between freedom as the universal and the absolute on the one hand, and the pursuit of happiness as the empirical, particularistic, merely personal on the other. It is now clear why one can accept the autonomy argument whatever one's philosophical conviction, if only one subscribes to autonomy as the major personal value, and why the same cannot be asserted about the universality argument. Let me repeat that the rejection of Kant's dual anthropology implies the rejection of his universality argument in *uno actu*, but not that of his autonomy argument.

However, the autonomy argument alone is too weak to serve as the basis for a modern political philosophy. The question of how political freedom is possible needs to be answered in both theoretical and practical terms, and the argument that freedom should be preferred to the pursuit of happiness on all counts is definitely not an answer to that question. However, one should add that, once the Kantian dualistic anthropology has been left behind, the question of how freedom is possible, which cannot be answered within the confines of the Kantian system, will not be raised. Nevertheless, we remain within the Kantian orbit because his concerns are ours. The question of how political freedom is possible remains speculative in part because possibility cannot be derived from past and present experience, and in part because the idea of freedom is by definition counterfactual. But we (men and women, a whole people, social classes, social systems, the human race) have accumulated a rich experience of political freedom, of the many interpretations of the value of freedom and their diversity. Should one assume with Kant that freedom is absolute and eternal (unchangeable), one must subject all interpretations of freedom to the universal maxim in order to test their validity. But if one assumes with Hegel that the abstract idea of freedom is being concretized through every interpretation and contestation, one can hardly surmise that it remains the same; one should rather assume that it changes while also remaining the same. It does not follow from this that all interpretations and contestations of freedom can be accepted as legitimate. As mentioned, the idea of freedom can be, and in fact often is, used as a tool to rob others of their freedom. This is far more true now than it was in Kant's time. Since the idea of freedom as an abstract idea has actually been universalized, it is this fact of history (the historically constituted fact of reason) that allows for a far greater variety of both lawful and unlawful interpretations of the idea. To conceive of modernity as the ongoing concretization of freedom is Hegel's theoretical innovation. Still, a limiting concept is needed, for without one we cannot distinguish between the lawful and the unlawful use of the idea of freedom in political contestation. My use of Kantian terminology here is intentional, because in my mind it was Kant who found the way to distinguish lawful from unlawful interpretations of freedom. The celebrated stipulation that one should never use other people as mere means qualifies for this task perfectly. If actions or institutions that result directly from an interpretation of freedom instrumentalize other persons in principle, the interpretation must be regarded as unlawful. In contemporary jargon, we would consider such an act as the ideological use of the idea of freedom.

The non-instrumentalization formula is actually the imperative of autonomy: we have thus arrived back at Kant's 'autonomy argument'. We have found the 'autonomy argument' too weak to advise us on the possibility of political freedom. Now we have come to the conclusion that it can offer a different kind of service. But if the non-instrumentalization formula alone can decide whether or not inter-pretations of freedom are lawful, if it can act as the supreme arbiter in matters of freedom, one cannot help but conclude that autonomy is the only common denominator of all liberties and freedoms. The universality argument is perhaps just an empty shell, because only autonomy, or rather the norm of autonomy, can be thought of as universal. Once this is accepted, we come to the conclusion that different interpretations of freedom do not need to be universal, nor do they need to be universalizable in order to become the cornerstones of political freedom. If an interpretation of freedom gets the green light from the non-instrumentalization formula, this very interpretation enters into a relationship with universality. The relationship with universality is, however, not necessarily a universal relationship. Political freedom is possible if several interpretations of freedom enter into a relationship with universality, yet only few of them, perhaps only a single one, will become a universal relationship.

IV

The postulate that no one should be made happy against their will makes perfect sense. The injunction that no one should be made free against their will sounds tautological and nonsensical. There is, however, no natural or logical element in either sentence that might account for their respective 'rationality' or 'irrationality'; it is only the dense network of our prejudgements (not prejudices) that determines the reasonableness of the first postulate and the tautological character of the second. 'Determining' is the appropriate expression here because the perception of the second postulate as tautological results from the commitment to freedom as autonomy, from the privileged position that this interpretation of freedom had started to assume in the modern world. Kant accepted the privileged position of autonomy among all other interpretations of freedom with a gesture. But he failed to draw all the conclusions from this gesture for strictly philosophical reasons, some of which I have briefly mentioned, as well as others that I must leave unmentioned.

There are three such possible conclusions from the foregoing. There is, first, the one I have briefly mentioned: a host of interpretations of freedom exist that, if meticulously followed as regulative ideas or actualized as constitutive ones, enrich and concretize freedom, without being universal or even open to universalization. All these could also be inferred from the statement of the privileged position of autonomy, for only its universality can grant autonomy its privileged position among all other interpretations of freedom. Second, all the interpretations of freedom that stand in the universal relationship without themselves being or becoming universal are, by definition, also particular and individual, that is, different. This point was made by Hegel and it is well taken. But in Kant's scenario, difference, particularity and individuality are all linked with happiness, not with freedom. Third, given that many interpretations of freedom that get the green light from the supreme arbiter, autonomy, still remain different, particular or even unique, they must include determinations of a kind that are summed up by Kant in the concept 'happiness'.

Moreover, at this point one cannot help but presuppose a need for freedom, or, rather, many different needs for freedoms of different kinds. To avoid misunderstanding: freedom is not a need, but an idea, and all interpretations of freedom are ideas on a greater or lesser level of generality. Yet freedom and all the interpretations thereof are *also* needs. Needs are related to values and, conversely, an ongoing interpretation of values guides claims for the recognition and for the satisfaction of needs. Interpretations of freedom arouse needs for freedom and, in turn, needs for freedom trigger new interpretations of freedom. True enough, needs for freedom can be extinguished once ideas are annihilated, but ideas cannot be extinguished even if needs have been rooted out because ideas are written on a slab of stone. This undeniable precedence of ideas over needs is, however, a meagre consolation for the advocates of dualistic anthropology given that evil maxims share the privilege.

Having rejected Kant's universality argument, we should recall its political message: freedom unties, happiness divides. If freedom, on the one hand, and need recognition and need satisfaction, on the other hand, cannot be disentangled, and this is what I have tried to show, should we then conclude that man is doomed to be a wolf to other men, and that the emergence of the universal idea of freedom did not change the rules of this primordial game in the slightest? I think that questions like this have nothing to do with our Kantian/anti-Kantian meditations. Though in my view Kant made too strong a case for the kingdom of ends, and he could not withstand the temptation of embarking on a mental experiment with a possible anthropological revolution, his universality argument in itself leaves the questions of empirical possibility wide open. In a similar fashion, I am not indulging in historical predictions either when I briefly advance ideas that I will elaborate at some length in the next essay, namely, that the non-dualistic concept of our race does not exclude the possibility of as much concord as is needed for the cooperation and the coexistence of people living under free constitutions. Whether the universalization of the value of freedom will change the rules of the primordial game remains to be seen. The issue to be addressed is under what conditions this rule can be changed, and not whether the wolf will turn into a lamb.

Assume for a moment that all people on our earth are organized in free republics and they subscribe to the three principles Kant so magnificently formulated. This has more likelihood now than in Kant's time, given that the three principles, once elaborated in full, have probably triggered certain needs for freedom in people who scarcely knew anything about man, citizen or burgher 200 years ago. The principles *qua* principles do not determine the character of any republic, they merely set the framework in which conflicts of needs and clashes between different interpretations of freedom can be settled. They also establish procedures to settle the conflicts and clashes by discourse and negotiation, instead of by violence and force. If conflicts and contestations within and among states could be settled in this fashion, even Kant's dream of perpetual peace could cease to be utter nonsense. This is the Utopia of a kind of concord that does not exclude discord, for conflicts are not eliminated, only the rules to act them out are changed. One can make a case for the possibility of a world where all people are bound together by ties of symmetric reciprocity alone, with or without a dualistic anthropology.

V

The anti-instrumentalization formula becomes politically constitutive if all people are tied to each other only by bonds of symmetric reciprocity. Kant was perfectly in tune with the script of political liberalism when he advised us to disregard moral motivations. The political efficacy of the non-instrumentalization formula depends not on the goodwill of the political actors, but on the norms and rules of their cooperative and conflict-solving procedures. However, such norms and rules are neither established nor observed (which amounts to the same thing in practice) if men and women remain mere bystanders and recipients in political contests. Full symmetric reciprocity in all political and social affairs is, of course, a counterfactual (a merely regulative) practical idea, but symmetric reciprocity in certain affairs or in certain concrete political bodies, big or small, is not. In order to make such an arrangement work, everyone concerned must enjoy not only the right, but also the possibility, of active participation. That Kant was reluctant to acknowledge this right has more to do with his times than with his philosophy. None the less, the fact that he disregarded the conditions of political action to the same extent as the conditions of morality is a flaw that follows directly from his dualistic anthropology.

Once again this is a territory where liberty and needs cannot be disentangled, but this time for heuristic reasons. I will enumerate a few issues to demonstrate my point, though space does not allow me to elaborate on them.

We cannot grant full recognition to each other without recognizing each other's needs as well. The kind of recognition that is due to the reason (rationality) of the other person alone is not the recognition of the other person at all. Symmetric reciprocity remains an empty idea unless we recognize the needs of all of us, with the exception of those needs whose satisfaction requires the use of other persons as mere means for reasons of principle.

As mentioned, the idea of freedom elicits the need for freedom; the need for freedom for its part elicits interpretations of the idea of freedom of various kinds and contents. Such interpretations are practical, for people concerned with one or the other issue interpret freedom in order to embrace the issue and legitimize it. Claims for the recognition and the satisfaction of our needs and those of others belong to such issues. The recognition of all needs (with the above proviso) is a major constituent of freedom. The satisfaction of all needs definitely is not: Kant is justified in this respect. However, one can say that the satisfaction of all needs is impossible in a modern, dynamic world and still claim that the satisfaction of certain needs must be acknowledged as the condition of political freedom.

Under conditions of dire poverty, lack of education or social discrimination, the conditions for practising freedoms are absent. Here we encounter needs whose satisfaction is constitutive of freedom itself. If we take the 'priority-of-autonomy' argument seriously, as we certainly do, we must come to the conclusion that needs that are connected with the possibility of practising freedom must be met. The non-instrumentalization formula advises us that no one should be made happy against their will. Whenever people, through no choice of their own but owing to the absence of the possibility of a considered choice, fail to participate in political and social contestations, they objectively let others choose for them, make them 'happy' or 'unhappy'. Paternalism, patriarchy and patronage – the main political evils in Kant's mind, evils he wanted to exorcise by purifying the concept of freedom of the divisive poison of happiness – return now even more powerfully, as the unacknowledged needs take their revenge.

One could level a good counter-argument against this line of thought. If certain kinds of needs should be met for the sake of freedom, why not others? What we consider the proper condition for participation in citizen actions is just a matter of perception. One can be a political agent under any conditions. Once we start talking about proper conditions, we will never know where to stop, and finally no condition will be good enough for the practice of citizen's duties. Such duties are unconditional, and who does not practise them forsakes his or her right to freedom by his or her own will. To this very sensible counter-argument one can only answer that citizens themselves decide in each case what should be regarded as a sufficient condition for practising citizenship and what should not. This is just another way of practising freedom. Second, although participating in citizen action is a duty as well as a right, it is also a need, even if not for all.

VI

In a footnote to *Perpetual Peace*,[11] Kant makes the suggestion that one should rather presuppose that nature and freedom work towards the same end than flatter tyrants and abuse the human race. This is as close as one can get to presenting a theoretical commitment as a value choice. The present essay has urged readers, whatever philosophical conviction they might otherwise cherish, to reconfirm Kant's suggestion in a more theory-free, but by no means value-free form. One should rather presuppose that men and women, as free political and social actors, can work towards the universalization of the relations of symmetric reciprocity than legitimize totalitarianism, nuclear suicide or technological barbarism.

Notes

1   John Rawls, *Theory of Justice* (London: Oxford University Press, 1972).
2   Immanuel Kant, *Critique of Pure Reason*.
3   'Speculative Beginning of Human History', in *Perpetual Peace and Other Essays*, translated by Ted Humphrey (Indianopolis: Hackett, 1983).
4   If not indicated otherwise, I am referring to Immanuel Kant, *Critique of Practical Reason* and *Foundation of the Metaphysic of Morals*.
5   Kant's political and historical essays concentrate on the discussion of these connections. They are collected in the volumes *Kant on History* (Indianapolis: Bobbs-Merrill, 1963) and Kant's *Political Writings* (Cambridge: Cambridge University Press, 1970).
6   Immanuel Kant, *Metaphysical Elements of Justice* (Indianapolis: Bobbs-Merrill, 1965). This is the English translation of the first part of *Metaphysik der Sitten*. The second part is translated into English as a separate volume, *The Doctrine of Virtue*, translated by Mary Gregor (Philadelphia: University of Pennsylvania Press, 1971).
7   *The Conflict of the Faculties*, in *Political Writings*.
8   The German term *Mensch* does not indicate gender. However, in this context it cannot properly be rendered but by the word 'man'.
9   Kant, *The Metaphysical Elements of Justice*.
10 Kant, 'What is Enlightenment?', in *Political Writings*.
11 In *Perpetual Peace and Other Essays*.

8
Rights, Modernity, Democracy

I

Modernity is a breakthrough in the process of deconstructing (in the sense of the German term *Abbauen*) the 'natural artifice' that for millennia had secured the survival of the human race. All great civilizations, from ancient Egypt to Mexico through medieval Europe, represented a version of the only socio-political arrangement that was able – until the emergence of modernity – to integrate men and women into an organized whole, beyond the pale of a (village) community and the natural ties of blood relationship. A few attempts were made to deconstruct the 'natural artifice' in order to set up an alternative arrangement, the best-known example being the Athenian democracy. However, until very recently, all of them failed.

I have termed the pre-modern socio-political arrangements versions of the 'natural artifice'. 'Natural' here stands for 'arrangement by nature' (*physis*) in the Aristotelian interpretation of the concept. Whatever is common to all socio-political arrangements exists 'by nature'. The term 'artifice' is the counterpoint to the term 'natural'. What is natural to the pre-modern conception is no longer natural to the modern one. Modern imagination begins to emerge when and where the 'natural' appears as artificial; a man-made construct that can be deconstructed.

A virtually infinite variety of arrangements is possible within the general mode of the natural artifice. What is common to all of them has become decisive only for us moderns. For the non-moderns it was the difference between the distinct natural artifices that mattered. Not even the early moderns aimed at the deconstruction of the natural artifice; rather they attempted to streamline, modify or perfect it. The deconstruction of one element was followed by the deconstruction of several others with increasing speed, until the aim of an *alternative* socio-political arrangement appeared on the horizon. The speed of deconstruction accelerated to such a degree that when it slows down, at least in the so-called Western world, the process is perceived to have stopped.

If we say, with Aristotle, that arrangements common to all political bodies and societies that are otherwise completely different in kind exist 'by nature', we can easily identify 'natural arrangements', with the sole exception of the project of modernity. I use the term 'the project of modernity' because in the actual, and very short, story of modernity a few vestiges of the ancient arrangements still survive, and in some cases remain well entrenched. For all practical purposes, the modern arrangement is completely unnatural. In spite of the radical deconstruction of the alternative arrangement, modernity has not yet proved its ability of a *longue durée* survival. It may or may not do so in the future. It is an open-ended arrangement, an experiment. Modernity could become an alternative social arrangement, and as such 'natural', under two conditions. First, if it succeeds in becoming a 'natural artifice' just like the one it has so successfully deconstructed. In other words, if it becomes natural arrangement in the Aristotelian sense (existing 'by nature', shared by each and every culture), that is, if it can accommodate at least as many versions of completely different concrete socio-political arrangements and cultures as did the first 'natural edifice'. Second, and this follows from the first, the longevity of the 'experiment' of modernity depends on whether or not it can generate the mechanisms for cultural–ethical reproduction, and, more importantly, human motives for this reproduction.

The modern world is frequently described as non-traditional and it is contrasted with the traditional, pre-modern world. The juxtaposition makes sense on a few counts, but not on several others. Since the natural artifice of pre-modern arrangements is the so-called time-honoured tradition, the deconstruction of this tradition is perceived as radically anti-traditional. Furthermore, since the modern world is open-ended, tradition has lost the power of absolute justification. Yet it is equally true that the modern world exhibits a hitherto unprecedented enthusiastic relation to 'tradition as such' (that is, to several different kinds of tradition, not just one of them). Simultaneously, modernity has been moving towards establishing its own traditions. Modernity

appears as the executioner of all traditions. Whenever cultural models
have been disentangled from their original socio-political settings,
moderns eagerly rush to reinterpret and assimilate them into their
new, and still unnatural, alternative socio-political arrangements. The
fact that traditional assets are sometimes treated as museum pieces is
another matter, and cannot be addressed in the framework of this
essay.

In his celebrated book *After Virtue*,[1] Alasdair MacIntyre makes the
apposite observation that traditional ethical (moral) terms are used out
of their original context in modernity. He adds to this that, having
been severed from their original setting, these terms no longer make
sense. True enough, most of our ethical terms were born out of the
pre-modern arrangement, though their philosophical interpretations
were mostly inspired by the Greek enlightenment. (As a result, these
terms may be more easily disentangled from their original setting than
certain other concepts.) However, free-floating cultural traditions gain
a new meaning within the framework of the new socio-political and
cultural patterns. It may well be true that we misunderstand these
ethical terms, or that we cannot understand them without adopting an
imaginary position in the arrangements of the 'natural artifice' of pre-
modernity. But this is not a 'truth' for us, for it neither edifies us nor
provides us with an essential insight. MacIntyre's statement draws its
pathos from the underlying assumption that modern men and women
will be unable to rearrange those ethical terms in their completely
different setting even after considerable interpretive modification.
MacIntyre is not the only one to mistake deconstruction for destruction.
For him, as for many others, modernity, this unnatural arrangement,
is by definition also barren. The deconstruction of the 'natural artifice'
is believed to go with the destruction of the whole of tradition: of all
beliefs, convictions, certainties, morals, religions, meaningful ways of
life. If one presupposes, as I do, that deconstruction is not destruction,
but rather a radical rearrangement of forms of human cooperation and
the mechanisms of problem-solving, the fact that traditional ethical
terms are free-floating, sometimes out of context, does not forebode
doom. One may still cherish the trust that, sooner or later, they will be
rearranged within the socio-political universe of symmetric reciprocity.

What was after all that famous 'natural' socio-political arrangement?
First and foremost, it meant the rule of a single male. In 99 per cent of
all human cultures (and this may still be a quantitative understatement),
this single male ruled uncontested. In society, that is, within the
family, in the *oikos*, this was the case even during the very short

148   *Rights, Modernity, Democracy*

periods of republican or democratic constitutions when a few males, instead of one, ruled in the political arena. The natural artifice is the arrangement of asymmetric reciprocity. Its world is hierarchically organized. The members of each cluster are equals among themselves, and they are all unequal in relation to the members of other clusters, higher or lower. One belongs to a social cluster even in the mother's womb; the destiny of the newborn is written upon the cradle. The famous teleological determination of virtues appertains to hierarchy and asymmetry. We may well be equals before God, but in this vale of tears we must live up to our own particular virtues, duties and destinies – those of the perfect master or the slave, of the nobleman or the serf, or of the obedient wife – according to the hierarchy of ends. This arrangement worked; sometimes fairly well.

In deconstructing this 'natural artifice', modernity has embarked on a unique historical experiment. Human coexistence is now to be renegotiated. In the prudent discussion of 'the social contract' or a 'new covenant', the early moderns found an apposite metaphor for this renegotiation. The term 'contract' is awkward, and it invokes unhappy associations, yet it still grasps the most crucial aspect of modernity. *Symmetric reciprocity* is the name of the new arrangement, at all levels – from the family to political decision-making through the relationship of cultures, peoples and states.

Symmetric reciprocity, as the main constitutive element of modern society, does not exclude a hierarchy resulting from the division of labour. However, men and women are not thrown into its network by birth; they enter into such a division later, potentially (although not really) by their own choice. Real inequality and formal equality are not contradictions. One is born equal and becomes unequal. One is born free and one can become unfree. Monarchy is the natural rule in a world of asymmetric reciprocity. Yet, sporadically, other political arrangements can also be accommodated. One can assume that democracy is the natural rule in a world of symmetric reciprocity; however, one cannot exclude the success of other political arrangements. In our age, totalitarianism emerged as an alternative political answer to modernity. The force of attraction of totalitarianism indicates, among other things, how strongly entrenched is the old ideal of a charismatic single male ruler.

In a society of asymmetric reciprocity, the worst tyranny is less dangerous than it is in our society. In an asymmetric society the hierarchy of the estates, the whole socio-political pyramid, protects the single person against the tyrant. No such protection exists within the arrangement of symmetric reciprocity. Total control and the totalization of the entire socio-political universe can come about only here and now.

It is too early to assess how successful the new arrangement is compared with the old. The new is pregnant with great promise, but it also harbours unpredictable dangers. Even if modernity survives and symmetric reciprocity takes democratic forms by opening up access to political decision-making, action and rule for everyone concerned, the world could still end up by becoming spiritless, lacking in culture, void of subject and deprived of meaning. However, these questions of the gravest importance are beyond the horizon of the present line of enquiry.

II

All this makes it essential to distinguish between the concept of natural *law* and that of natural *right*. In his discussion of natural rights in pre-modern times, Leo Strauss, in his book *Natural Right and History*,[2] merges 'natural law' and 'natural right' theories in order to contrast both with historicism. But I am convinced that the historical circumstance in which historicism came to be opposed to both concepts is not a sufficient reason to identify them.

Concepts of natural law are very well placed in the framework of the 'natural artifice'. If all customs as well as social or political institutions that happen to be shared by all integrations exist 'by nature', one can easily draw the conclusion that the common aspect of socio-political arrangements is that they are what they are by the 'law of nature'. Like all legitimizing devices, the conception of 'natural law' also allows for a critical use, as can be seen in the case of Antigone. One can have recourse to this device in claiming justice. In other words, certain well-defined rights derive from the law of nature. But the old concept of natural law cannot be used as a tool for deconstructing the natural artifice itself, unless 'natural law' is interpreted in the light of so-called 'natural rights'. For it is the idea of 'human rights', the archetype of natural rights, that upsets the time-honoured balance of asymmetric reciprocity by challenging it head-on.

Hegel dismissed the natural right theory as a fiction[3] in order to replace it with yet another fiction. But Hegel's argument deserves closer scrutiny. In terms of this argument, statements such as 'man is born free' or 'all men are born free' are not only false but also guilty of reasserting the ontology of the old 'natural law'. In the old theory, Hegel ruminates, free men are free because they are thus born, slaves are slaves also because they are thus born, and so on. In stating that we are all free because we all are thus born, we entrench ourselves in a false ontology. In fact, we are not born free but we can nevertheless become free; this is the truth of our age, Hegel contends.

However, statements such as 'all men are born free' need not be unmasked as fictions, because they are meant to be fictions (or metaphors). Their ontological character is illusory. *They are ethical and political principles.* They are *not theoretical*, but rather pure practical principles. The first part of Rousseau's famous dictum gains its political weight from its counterpoint contained in the second part: 'Men are born free – and everywhere they are in chains.'[4] It is not an explanatory, but rather a politico-rhetorical device. The Kantian distinction between regulative and constitutive theoretical principles on the one hand, and regulative and constitutive practical principles on the other, was a sophisticated philosophical rendering of actual ethical and political practices. The famous principles of the Declaration of Independence, which, in terms of the text, were held to be self-evident truths, illuminate how such principles are used practically both in regulating action and in constituting a new socio-political arrangement, in other words, a constitution.

The same aspects of 'natural right' theories that were criticized by Hegel could also be considered a merit on several counts. First, 'natural right' theories use pre-modern devices ('man is born such and such') in order to upset the pre-modern *status quo ante*; and this is indeed a debit. However, it can be transformed into a credit if it is well done. Deconstruction, from ancient sophism through post-modern practices, prefers to upset time-honoured ideas, customs and ideologies from within, on their own grounds, without using any further presuppositions. Yet 'human (natural) right' theories do not stop at this stage. The moment they use rights as an *arche*, they take an external position. And at this point we again face Hegel's disapproval. Principles are empty Oughts, he contends, if they have no actuality. And indeed, if men are everywhere in chains, the 'self-evident truth' that men are born free has no actuality at all. By way of conclusion, one can only utter the seemingly empty sentence that men *ought* to be free. Without entering this complex and rhetoric-ridden debate, I am inclined again to credit the 'human (natural) right' theory with at least an inkling of two great intuitions. First, the claim that men ought to be what they are (namely free) is a streamlined reformulation of the

Aristotelian attempt to unify *physis* and *nomos*. However, this time the unity is based – and this is the line of division between the 'natural artifice' and modernity – on an arrangement of symmetric reciprocity. Second, the theory suggests that agreement and disagreement in theoretical–speculative matters and agreement/disagreement on the practical plane can be entirely separated from one another. The significance of this second great intuition needs to be explored in some detail.

Let us recapitulate Rousseau's logic: all men are born free; yet they are everywhere in chains; they ought to be free (unity of *physis* and *nomos*). Obviously, here Ought is not inferred from Is. The sentence 'all men are born free' is a value statement. Closest to a statement of fact comes rather the second sentence 'they (men) are everywhere in chains'. Whether or not this statement of fact is true is irrelevant from the normative point of view. As far as the norm is concerned, men simply should be what they by nature are, namely, free. One could continue to discuss the truth content of the statement 'men are everywhere in chains'. One could first dismantle its rhetoric, and figure out afterwards who is free and who is unfree, what makes some freer than others, under what conditions people can be freer than they now are, and so on. One could also continue to disagree on all points. To cut a long story short: the recognition of the diversity of opinions is built into the original stance of the human right concept. Philosophers, being for the most part uneasy with open-ended dialogues, did what they could to hide from the public eye this 'blot on the escutcheon' – the permissiveness, the pluralism and the practical liberalism that are inherent in the concept of human right.

The value statement 'all men are born free' is both a descriptive and an expressive statement. It can be read as follows: we hold it to be a self-evident truth that men are born free; it is precisely because of this shared conviction that men are, indeed, born free. And this is a true statement. For if all men hold it to be a self-evident truth that all men are born free, then in fact all men are thus born. Put bluntly, the status of all men will be one of 'freely born'. As 'freely born' ones, all human beings will have an equal status at the moment of their birth. The sentence is simply the expression of the new socio-political arrangement, and this is precisely why it can serve as the best means (as well as the best battle-cry) for deconstructing the old.

Those who challenge the truth content of that self-evident truth ('all men are born free') on the grounds of the unequal distribution of wealth pinpoint a burning social issue but misunderstand the statement they believe they are undermining. Among the free-born men of Athens, some were rich and others poor, some were the offspring of good families, others came from families of ill repute. But they were all born free, whereas others were born slaves. The famous battle-cry has spelled out the absolute difference between the natural artifice and the new (modern) arrangement. Slavery is an anomaly in modernity, whereas the unequal distribution of wealth is not. The latter is the matter that needs to be addressed within the framework of the new arrangement, and it is to be addressed in different ways within different forms of life.

If some (not all) people are freely born, their freedom is determined by the very existence of those born unfreely. What they can do and others cannot is what 'being born freely' means. If every human being is freely born, the concrete content of having been freely born disappears. Freedom becomes an abstraction, an empty possibility. This is why the question of what freedom is needs to be raised. The answers to this question are almost infinite, and they are eminently practical. Modernity is about the concretization of 'freedom'. Every form of life in modernity is by definition the concretization of the abstract possibility of having been born free. This is meant not as a predictive, rather as an analytical statement. There is no longer a 'social pyramid'. The modern world is flat because it is symmetrical. This is precisely why modern values can be universal. The universality of a value is a perfectly simple thing. It means that the opposite of the value cannot be chosen as a value. Freedom is certainly such a universal value, since no one is publicly committed to unfreedom as a value. The value of life also comes close to attaining a universal status.

At the moment of their conception, universal values became the main objects of enthusiasm. This is the story of the French Revolution and Kant's philosophy. The idea of freedom still triggers enthusiasm, particularly in moments of liberation. But where modernity is taken for granted and when it has reached its adequate political form (one or another type of democracy), enthusiasm recedes, and the work of concretization of the universal value(s) takes off.

Rights are the institutionalized forms of the concretization of universal values (both of the value of freedom and that of life). They can be substantive or procedural. Allegorically speaking, they can establish frameworks for action, negotiation and much else as well, as they serve as roadsigns for steps taken in the direction of the further 'concretization' of values.

Right-language is, and should be, the *lingua franca* of modern democracy, which, in contrast to the ancient model, includes liberalism. Right-language cannot achieve full meaning if it is spoken from the position of the 'natural artifice'. Symmetric reciprocity is the condition of the mastery of this language. But right-language cannot be a mother-tongue. The mother-tongue is the lingo of forms of life. More forms of life give rise to greater differences and more mother-tongues. Yet right-language is not a second language and it is certainly not an artificial one. One learns it together with the mother-tongue, but it is spoken only if the occasion so requires.

Let me emphasize once again that modernity is a newborn, and that modern democracy is still in its first experimental stage. We do not know how things are going to develop, but we can give voice to certain concerns. Should right-language be raised to the status of a mother-tongue, no real differences could be accommodated in the modern world. Life would not merely be uniform, but also devoid of creative imagination. In addition, it would be a life without community and immediacy. And the converse also seems true: if right-language is not generally spoken as a *lingua franca*, modernity might easily go down in the history books (if there still are any) as yet another misguided and miscarried experiment of *homo sapiens*.

III

Rights are formal and abstract, but not in the same way or to the same extent as universal values are. They always include a substantive element ('freedom for what, in what, to what', and so on). These substantive elements are inherited from our ancestors. Referring to rights means to claim something that is due, which is justice. The concept of rights stems from the concept of justice, but they are different in kind.

In my book *Beyond Justice*,[5] I have distinguished between the two main types of justice: static justice and dynamic justice.

Static justice is the perfect case of what I have termed the formal concept of justice: the norms and rules that constitute a human cluster should be applied consistently and continuously to each and every member of that cluster. Members of the same cluster are constituted as equals by the very norms and rules that apply to them, while members who belong to different and interrelated clusters are constituted as unequals, given that different norms and rules apply to them. If clusteral norms are applied continuously and consistently, everyone gets what is due to him or her. Since rules and norms define with a certain precision what is due to whom, no conflict arises about the conception of the distribution of honours, things and services, only about their actual distribution. People do not claim 'rights' in claiming what is due to them; rather, they claim satisfaction.

In the case of dynamic justice, certain norms and rules themselves are declared unjust. The claimants or contesters want a 'new deal', a new set of norms or rules to be substituted for the old ones. In so far as they aim at delegitimizing actual norms and rules, they have recourse to values, in particular to those of freedom and life. Normally, delegitimizing claims do not play first fiddle. The matter is decided by violence or, at best, by negotiations backed by force.

In modernity, dynamic justice has become an everyday phenomenon. Since daily life cannot be the territory of constant street fights, alternative solutions have been sought, and dynamic justice proved to be a fertile heritage. Delegitimizing and legitimizing claims alike began to play the role of first fiddle in the process of conflict-resolution.

The same story can also be recounted in reverse. Once it has become a self-evident truth that all men are born free, everything that is due to free persons is due to all persons. What is due to free persons traditionally? First, the maximum protection of the law, if there is any; second, access to communal political decision-making if it is common practice. Hence, if everyone is born free, everyone has to be equal before the law and receive maximum protection under the law. Furthermore, everyone needs to have equal access to institutions of political and communal decision-making. Yet equal and maximum protection by the law and equal access to power are never completely realized. Old wounds reopen, and completely unforeseen problems emerge. Apart from everything else, basic political and legal categories are the main training ground of hermeneutics. What seems to be a fair amount of proteciton, equality or political power today will appear as ridiculously unsatisfactory tomorrow. Interpretation guided by dynamic justice becomes a matter of course, a daily practice.

Whenever men and women argued on behalf of alternative rules and norms, they had recourse to values such as freedom and life. Since dynamic justice is a matter of course and needs to be constantly practised, it has to take institutionalized forms. The procedure of having recourse to such values as freedom or life also needs to follow certain basic patterns. It is the right-language that provides these patterns.

Thus right-language performs a double task. it is the major vehicle for deconstructing the natural artifice from the standpoint of symmetric reciprocity. It is also the language of conflict-management within the socio-political arrangement of symmetric reciprocity. In the first capacity, it has an air of nobility. In the second capacity it is but a tool, an equation, having a purely instrumental value. And yet it is in this second capacity that right-language can become *natural* in the ancient sense, that is, as something common to all cities, states and peoples. Ancient travellers from Herodotus to Marco Polo knew that wherever they visited so-called 'civilized' countries they would meet persons born to rule and others born to obey. They merely had to find out who were the ones born to rule and those born to obey, and, further, which were the forms of ruling and obeying. Under a possible natural arrangement of symmetric reciprocity, cultures may well differ from each other to the same extent as, in Marco Polo's time, China differed from Venice. The 'only' change would be that the truth that all men *and women* are born free would be taken as self-evident in each of them.

IV

Alasdair MacIntyre, in his latest book *Whose Justice? Which Rationality?*[6] plays the best and, as far as I can see, the only unbeatable trump card against liberalism in general, and against right-language in particular. McIntyre's argument is that by emphasizing difference or by subscribing to total cultural and epistemological relativism one merely reconfirms all the fundamental claims of liberalism. As long as one believes in a community of discourse, where discourse is conducted according to neutral, impersonal, tradition-independent standards, every concrete language can be translated into this common language. This is one way of easily accommodating each and every 'difference'. Once this illusion is abandoned by post-Enlightenment persons, all everyday worlds are treated as distinct and unique examples of pragmatic necessities and every framework of all-embracing belief extended beyond the realm of pragmatic necessity will be regarded as equally unjustified. The post-Enlightenment liberal views the order of traditions as a series of masquerades. Theirs are the internationalized languages of modernity, 'the languages of everywhere and nowhere'.[7] Only an *absolutist* language, the language of a particular form of life that claims full rightness and truth for itself, presents a real, *not merely philosophical but also social*, alternative to an all-encompassing liberal universe.

I think that this is a correct assumption. Every view and each form
of life can be accommodated by liberalism except 'absolute absolutism'.
Absolutists claim that only the particular kind of truth they acknowledge
is true, only the kind of action they recommend is proper, virtuous or
right, while all alternative views and practices are either untrue or
wrong. Absolutism finds an easy accommodation within liberalism:
moreover, liberalism itself frequently takes an absolutist shape.
'Absolute absolutism' makes the same statements as absolutism, yet it
denies (to repeat: *not merely philosophically but also socially*) the right
of others (other absolutists and relativists alike) to make a similar claim
for the truth and rightness of their own theory or practice. This is why
'absolute absolutism' cannot be accommodated by sincere liberalism.
In addition, absolute absolutism is the language of the 'natural artifice',
whereas the 'right-language' is one of the major tools for deconstructing
this artifice.

I coined the term 'sincere liberalism' in order to juxtapose it with
'insincere liberalism'. Liberalism becomes insincere if it pretends to be
able to accommodate absolute absolutism. Just recently, in the wake of
the Rushdie affair, we witnessed a less than edifying display of
insincere liberalism. A liberalism that maintains that, since all cultures
are unique and they need to be respected in their uniqueness, one must
be 'understanding' towards the specificity of exterminating ideological
enemies and one should practise tactful tolerance towards the call for
ideological murder is not liberalism but simply a bad joke. 'Right-
language' is, as a rule, drab and commonsensical. Yet sometimes
courage is needed to talk this language, and the need for the old
enthusiasm may recur. The readiness to display the old-fashioned
enthusiasm is one of the major characteristics of sincere liberalism. In
a political context, sincere liberalism is *democratic liberalism*.

It is difficult to remain true to sincere or democratic liberalism as
long as one juxtaposes the 'right-language' with historicism. Philosophy as
a merely speculative enterprise can produce marvels with transcend-
entalism. However, speaking the 'right-language' is not a theoretical,
but rather a pragmatic, practical and judgemental exercise. Here
transcendental deductions are not conclusive. For my part, I have
recommended the introduction of the historical dimension into
speculations about so-called universals on the theoretical–philosophical
plane; but this issue is extraneous to the concerns of this essay. Put
briefly, the 'right-language' need not present itself as *the* rational
language of the human race beyond space, time and history, nor
should it make a (fraudulent) plea for total impartiality. Commitment

to the 'right-language' does not need to be combined with the belief that rational argumentation leads to the victory of the best argument without any other conditions having been met. Since the 'right-language' is not the embodiment of *logos*, those who think that it needs to become the *lingua franca* of our age are not logocentrist. Making the recommendation for the 'right-language' is a very general commitment to the modern world as the world of symmetric reciprocity. The 'right-language' can be termed a historical and conditional universal (it is conditional because absolute absolutists do not speak this language). No commitment to any concrete form of life is implied in speaking the 'right-language' as the *lingua franca*; but a commitment to rejecting several forms of life is certainly implied. Democratic liberalism can embrace all metaphysico-ontological claims, all kinds of sciences, creeds, vocations, plays, eccentricities. But it cannot shelter all practical (political and ethical) institutional arrangements, practices, judgements, exercises. In the same way that natural (human) right theories once deconstructed the old 'natural artifice' in the political theatre of the West, so right-language continues to deconstruct systems of asymmetry, whether they reappear in traditional forms or assume a certain new, streamlined shape. From totalitarianism to patriarchy, from group discrimination to all kinds of institutionalized subservience, the 'right-language' continues to challenge all principles, institutions and arrangements of asymmetric reciprocity.

V

Rights are first and foremost vehicles of conflict-resolution, although they also contribute to the emergence of certain conflicts and to their expression. Let me briefly illustrate the situation in which the 'right-language' needs to be spoken and how the language works through a model.

Let us assume that there are thousands and thousands of different cultures on our planet. Let us also assume that each of them speaks a mother-tongue that is untranslatable into the mother-tongue of any other. They are all unique. One culture is pluralistic, another is not; one is individualistic, another communitarian. They subscribe to different scientific paradigms, religions, artistic practices. One form of life acclaims the work ethic, another prefers leisure; one of them cultivates monogamy, another promiscuity. Actions that are regarded as completely rational within one form of life will be viewed as entirely irrational in another.

Let us further assume that there are certain conflicts between those cultures; this much, on the basis of historical experience, we may reasonably assume. Conflicts can be resolved by violence, force, negotiation and discourse. In order to negotiate and to conduct a discourse, a common language needs to be spoken. Since all the cultures in our model speak but their own language, and since this language cannot be translated into any other, negotiation and discourse are by definition excluded. What remains is violence and force. Put bluntly, in the case of a conflict, the stronger exterminates or enslaves the weaker. With a few exceptions, this is the way intercultural conflicts were solved in pre-modern times. Moral exhortation apart, this solution is no longer feasible; at least not in the long run. Owing to the modern development of industrial technology, both war and control have become total. If men and women who inhabit those entirely different cultures do not want to commit collective suicide, they must embrace the two remaining alternatives: negotiation and discourse. In order to negotiate or to conduct a discourse, they need to talk to one another. In order to talk to one another, they need a common language. No culture can superimpose its own language on all others. Given their complete difference, other cultures would not accept the offer (absolute absolutism). What remains is to invent a *lingua franca* spoken by every culture as its second language. It is not necessary that the whole mother-tongue of all cultures should be translated into this *lingua franca*, only the portion that enables citizens of each and every culture to address their conflicts in practical terms, to seek a solution together. This is how they invent the 'right-language'.

But right-language is never the starting point. These cultures cannot possibly invent right-language as their *lingua franca* without first having something in common. What they first need to have in common is the arrangement of symmetric reciprocity; or, as a minimum condition, they all need to accept as a self-evident truth that all human beings are born free.

Theoretically, we have maneouvred ourselves into a circle. But, in practice, there are no circles; there are no pure models either. There is no 'yes' or 'no', only a 'more' or a 'less'.

Although moving in circles is the headache of theory, not of political practice, here a formidable problem has remained that causes a headache for both theory and practice. The assumption that all the cultures, in themselves unique, of our pure model can address their conflicts in the language of rights does not imply that they can also solve their problems by using this language. In so far as they can, we are speaking in terms of rational compromise. Yet sometimes two rights are on a collision course. If this happens, an intercultural discourse has to discuss the very 'language of rights' in order to provide a new schema of interpretation. Intercultural discourse can actually be conducted with the mediation of an interpreter. All cultures in a discourse situation can make reference to their own values as ones embedded in their own form of life. The aim of such a discourse is consensus on an entirely new intercultural arrangement. I have described such a discursive procedure in my books *Radical Philosophy* and *Beyond Justice*,[8] and space does not allow for its recapitulation in this context. Yet what needs still to be emphasized is the very condition of the possibility of such a consensus, *which is a higher-order consensus prior to the discourse*. At this point it does not suffice to subscribe to freedom as a value and to the self-evident statement that all men are born free. It is equally necessary to accept that freedom is the highest (supreme) value. We are thus back at the circle, though on a higher level.

The age of philosophy of history confronted us with the choice between everything or nothing. Everything became nothing. But nothing did not become everything, only something. Rights are far from being everything – but they are certainly something.

Notes

1 Alasdair MacIntyre, *After Virtue: A Study in Moral Theory* (Notre Dame: University of Notre Dame Press, 1984).
2 Leo Strauss, *Natural Right and History* (Chicago: University of Chicago Press, 1965).
3 G. W. F. Hegel, *Philosophy of Right* (New York: Oxford University Press, 1967).
4 Jean-Jaques Rousseau, *The Social Contract* (New York: St Martin's Press, 1978).
5 Agnes Heller, *Beyond Justice* (Oxford: Blackwell, 1987).
6 Alasdair MacIntyre, *Whose Justice? Which Rationality?* (London: Duckworth, 1988).
7 MacIntyre, *Whose Justice?* pp. 395–6.
8 Agnes Heller, *Radical Philosophy* (Oxford: Blackwell, 1984).

9
Moses, Hsüan-tsang and History

I

In his magnificent essay, *Moses and Monotheism*,[1] Freud engaged in speculation about the wondrous deliverance from perdition, right after their birth, of heroes who were destined to be protagonists of myths. Among the numerous, although finite, number of motifs that are normally combined into a few typical patterns in such stories, Freud, in a quest for the 'truth' about Moses, focuses on three mythological constants. First, Moses, unlike Oedipus, was abandoned not in order to die but in order to live. Second, he was 'fished out of water' (not rescued from a desert or a cliff). Third, he was brought up by another family, yet he was to find his way back to his 'real' family. As is well known, Freud inferred from the combination of these mythological patterns that Moses had been an Egyptian who had tried to implant the then-suppressed monotheistic cult of Egypt among the rough and crude people of Israel. This bold interpretation is not the topic of the current essay; rather I shall consider the implications of Freud's method. Freud assumed that there was, there had to be, a complete fit between mythological language and historical truth. If the same motif reappears in two mythological narratives, it definitely stands for the same historical or 'real' stories or facts. This 'fit' can be deciphered once we familiarize ourselves with patterns of distortion, reversal and subterfuge – the work of our unconscious.

In recent decades of this century, myths have once again become topical for our self-understanding. But the approach to myths, from Lévi-Strauss to Blumenberg, has changed and diversified. Although the interpretation of bygone ages or the exploration of paradisiacal or less than paradisiacal islands attract our interest just as they did before, the main motivation for this enquiry needs to be sought in different quarters. It is not above all the unconscious self of the individual or the unexplored Id of the human species that we desire to decipher in a roundabout way. It is rather our history, our being here-and-now, the meaning of our own historical existence, that is put on the theoretical agenda with great urgency. One could associate the Freudian approach to myth with the historical consciousness of modernity, and our contemporary approaches with the historical consciousness of post-modernity. The latter will be the topic as well as the standpoint of the following enquiry.

One can understand myths as configurations of significations rather than as signs that indicate something else (the historical truth). Actually myths carry truth and/or untruth irrespective of the historical truth to which they may or may not be connected. We are ignorant of whether or not there was a historical figure behind the myth of Achilles. Yet this seemed irrelevant for Alexander the Great, much as it did later for Shakespeare. For Alexander the myth was true, for Shakespeare it was blatantly untrue, yet, for both, the 'message of the myth' was supremely relevant. In this respect, truth in myth resembles truth in philosophy.

Moses was fished out of water and brought up in the court of the Pharaoh. This is why Freud arrives at the conclusion that he was in fact the son of the Pharaoh's daughter. But if myths have their own truth, one cannot establish a direct connection between myth and historical reality. For myth *is* a reality. Stories of heroes of divine origin have been passed on since time immemorial. The man of extraordinary deeds, who spoke with authority, who promised deliverance and kept his promise, *deserved* a myth, and the myth was indeed bestowed upon him by contemporaries or successors. We have no knowledge of how and when the myth of Moses was bestowed upon 'the man Moses'. But we can be fairly certain that, although he spoke with absolute authority about his mission and his encounter with God, he did not believe that he had been put out in a basket on the river Nile as a newborn. Nor did Jesus of Nazareth know anything about the three kings and the star. First comes a mission, then the miracle.

A Chinese novel, *The Journey to the West*,[2] tells us the miraculous story of Hsüan-tsang, who travelled from China to the Western Heaven where he was presented to Buddha in the heavenly court. There he received the Scriptures and became a Buddha himself. The

Hsüan-tsang of the myth was born to Lady Ying, an unfortunate woman, whose husband was murdered by a knave who immediately usurped the husband's place, threatening to kill the lady's unborn child if she was unwilling to abide by his desires. When the boy was born, Lady Ying fastened him to a plank and put the plank on the river to save the child's life. She also cut his little toe and her little finger, and pinned a letter, written in her own blood, to the boy's garment. The river delivered the boy to a monastery where he was brought up by the monks. As a youth he searched for his mother, found her and avenged the murder of his father (who had already been resurrected) – and so on *ad libitum*. What a treasure-trove for Freudian speculation this story is! Except that this time we know the real story, to the extent that real stories can be known. Hsüan-tsang was born into a family of high Chinese officials. He became a Buddhist monk and decided to travel to India (to the West) in order to get hold of certain fundamental Buddhist scriptures. Since the Emperor did not give him permission to leave, he embarked secretly on the journey. After spending sixteen years in India, he returned home, and – with his nineteen translations and many original writings – marked a new beginning in the story of Chinese Buddhism.

The myth of Hsüan-tsang reminds us of the myth of Moses on several counts. And yet no similarities between the 'real' stories can be inferred from the similarities of the myths. Mythical elements are indeed up for grabs, but they cannot be conferred on just anyone. Men and women must deserve their myths. And certain elements fit one particular historical role better than another.

II

Myths are bestowed retrospectively. The owl of Minerva is after all a mythological bird and was borrowed as such by Hegel to serve as the metaphor of philosophy. The myth is conferred upon someone or something as the intersubjective authentication of the truth of a message that has already been heard.

We are not familiar with the 'real' story of Moses, whereas we are with the real story of Hsüan-tsang. But we do not need to be familiar with them in order to decipher some common Truth from the respective myths. Both stories are about a 'new beginning' in the life of a religion, a land and a people, bestowed upon the religious hero by the people in whose land the religion has been newly implanted (or rejuvenated and reformed). The river divides land from land, and whoever is fished out of the water brings new tidings. It is the language of the myth (of the past, the tradition) that makes the strongest stagement about those new tidings.

Similarly, it was the language of the past, of a tradition, that made the strongest statement about the entirely new tidings that had been conveyed by the French Revolution. Naturally, I have in mind the language of philosophy. The philosophy of history was merely the intersubjective authentication of the message that a new world had been born in the land of Europe, and that this world was the harbinger of glad tidings for the whole human race.

Just as heroes, prophets or saints deserve their myths (or else the myths would not be bestowed upon them), the modern world too deserved its philosophy of history. However, the language of philosophy and the language of mythology are different in kind. Their functional equivalence (as that of spiritual agencies that bestow meaning on agents) does not provide sufficient ground for equating them. If philosophies of history were myths, we could not account for their rapid demise before our eyes. Whatever has happened to the people of Israel, this has not affected the myth of the man Moses. Whatever has happned in our modern world has, however, quickly and deeply affected the truth of our paradigmatic narratives. They turned out to be self-dissolving narratives.

Philosophy was transformed into a depersonified narrative by Aristotle and has remained so ever since. Its protagonists are not men and women but concepts. Ancient recipients still had difficulty in coping with the depersonification of the language game. This is why they attributed miraculous stories to philosophers, and endowed them with the paraphernalia of mythological features, such as wisdom, cunning, superhuman continence or subhuman brutishness. Of those myths, only that of Socrates has remained intact. The rest is gone. In modern philosophy of history, depersonification has been consummated. No wonder, then, that the first onslaught against philosophies of history was related to the attempt to personify philosophy. I have in mind here Kierkegaard and, above all, Nietzsche. Since this attempt has so far failed to open up a new avenue in philosophy, even though it may yet do so, I am not going to return to it. This futility, and not the overlooking of important phenomena, brings me to the statement that philosophy, in contrast with myth, remains for the time being stubbornly apersonal and, in this sense, Aristotelian.

Hans Blumenberg, in his innovative explorations, confronts modern men and women with their own mythologies.³ Moderns, as much as pre-moderns, have forged a host of mythological stories and parables. In so doing they have used, sometimes lavishly, traditional mythological materials while reshaping and recasting them. Modern myths, no less than old ones, focus on 'great men'. Among others, Blumenberg discusses the Napoleon myths, in particular the representative narratives related to the encounter of the two 'great men', Napoleon and Goethe at Erfurt. Although the modern era is extremely attached to hero worship, none the less hero worship does not yield stories that would qualify as foundational narratives and that could bestow intersubjective authentication on the new times. The reasons for this are manifold. Let me mention only one of them. The modern age is future-oriented: the patina of longevity does not attain to the aura of sanctity in the field of acting and doing. Rather, it does so in the field of collecting and remembering. The institutions of modern liberalism and democracy are far from being charismatic. In addition, the short-lived charismatic institutions of the twentieth century, all linked to the worship of totalitarian dictators, have taught us a lesson about the dangerous consequences of the institionalization of charisma under the circumstance of future-orientation. Simultaneously, they have contributed to the demise of the great legitimizing philosophical narratives of modernity.

Hegel was a great admirer of Napoleon; once he termed the emperor 'the World Spirit on horseback'. But it would never have occurred to him to put his philosophy into the emperor's mouth or to make the dictator a protagonist of this philosophy in any sense. No man, not even the greatest, can be considered the *founder* of modernity; unlike Athens, modernity has no Theseus. For disagreement has been a constitutive element of modernity since its 'foundation'; universalism and pluralism presuppose one another by definition. To use the language of Hegel, the universal establishes itself first as an abstraction, and it is only history as difference, as conflict, as resolve and negation, this painful process of concrete determinations, that will fill the universal form with contents. The abstract forms, the process, the series of conflicts, are not founded; they just happen, unfold, grow and proceed. One of the reasons philosophy of history became so strongly foundationalist is that it denied the philosophical relevance of political foundation.

The universalistic claims of philosophies of history already mark their difference from myths. Despite disclaimers of their universality, for example in the form of singling out particularistic views, images or interests behind the universalistic façade, a philosophy of history cannot be unmasked as a new myth – this is how and why the term 'ideology' has been invented and put to critical or derogative use.

As mentioned, there is a similarity between the truth/untruth of a myth and that of a philosophy. Neither myth nor philosophy can be falsified, but we can turn away from both of them. In so far as we do so, they become untrue. However, as long as we make painstaking efforts to show that they are untrue, they are not entirely untrue. They must still be true for someone else, or otherwise why the effort? They *become* completely untrue when neither the evaluative term 'true' nor that of 'untrue' is applicable to them any more. For example, for a long time we have not applied the terms truth/untruth to the story of Zeus and Kronos.

But as the example itself indicates, mythological truth, in an odd and unexpected fashion, can be shifted into another medium. When a human group that had distinct religious or secular stories of foundation is gone for good, the mythical message of its stories also disappears for good. But mythological narratives are, or at least can be, 'representative stories' or parables (where 'representative' means: representative also for other groups). As 'typical' stories, they encapsulate human imagination more generally or universally than does the hero of a religion or people on whom the story happened to be bestowed. These stories remain with us in the form of images, visions and puns, which live their afterlife mostly in the aesthetic medium. 'Afterlife' means (virtual) immortality. Stories with an afterlife can always be recalled from the collective memory. This is how they become 'culture'. Can we expect that the same will happen to the representative narratives of philosophy of history?

One expects myths to be remote from facts and modern stories to be inclined to factuality. The picture is, however, more complex. Myths do not recognize the difference between fact, interpretation and fiction, though believers in myths sometimes do. Since rationalist cultures distinguish between reality and fiction irrespective of how far they divide reality itself into a 'lower' and a 'higher' kind, myths that appear in a fairly rational setting require faith from the believer. For this reason, Christianity needed a *credo*, while Judaism did not. To have faith means to take everything that happens in the myth for a fact, suspending the practice of distinguishing reality from fiction in the sphere of supreme reality. Philosophies of history, as offsprings, advocates and bards of the modern age, are stubborn rationalists in the above sense. Sympathetic recipients of a philosophy of history are supposed not to believe in it but to understand it, as well as to accept the relevance of its reasoning. But – and this is an important but – the 'authenticating narratives' of the modern (new) age (the ones that lend it authority) do not claim factuality in the same manner as did religious or political myths. Kant, who (together with Rousseau) stood at the beginning of the very short career of the great narratives, was the most outspoken here. For him, the distinction between fact and fiction was the hallmark of sound philosophical knowledge. So he termed his own philosophy of history a fiction, but a fiction with the noblest veneer, which makes us understand history, this enigmatic process, which remains inaccessible to perception and so also to mere theoretical understanding. Kant's fiction presents history as a progressive development that unfolds in the direction of the modern age. The Hegelian adventure of the World Spirit was not consciously meant to be a fiction, but neither was it meant as the reconstruction of factuality. To a lesser extent, this is also true of Marx's story of production, class struggle, alienation and the end of pre-history.

All these narratives meticulously follow the pattern of traditional metaphysics, constantly distinguishing between two levels of reality: the lower and the higher one. What is real at the lower level is not really, only seemingly, real. What is really real is essential and actual, and it is placed on the upper level. It is the metaphysical (strictly philosophical) tradition that allows philosophies of history to accept the rationalist tradition (the distinction between reality and fiction) on the one hand, and to tell, in the manner of myths, a fictitious story as a real one on the other. Philosophies of history appeal to our reason and not to our faith. And, yet, without a kind of faith one cannot subscribe to their particular division of reality into a lower and a higher sphere.

The relation between higher reality, fiction and factuality in philosophies of history cannot be addressed here. The problem is approached by almost each philosophy in a unique way, and space does not allow me to elaborate on them. But all of them agree on four points – regardless of whether they claim that they have recounted the story of world history 'as it really happened' or whether they affirm instead that only the stories fitted into their account deserve mention and will be recollected in human memory. First, they agree that history is universal; second, that it shows an eventual tendency to progress; third, that modernity is the consummation of that progressive development; and, lastly, that everything that has happened, is happening and is going to happen can be fitted smoothly into the universal framework of progression-towards-modernity, provided that the event in question is not contingent. The fourth idea can be formulated the other way around: every non-contingent event leads towards the consummation of the development of world history.

III

I have already referred once to the common experience of the generation that grew up during or after the Second World War: we all saw the great narratives of philosophy of history collapse or slowly disintegrate before our eyes. Valhalla on fire, the twilight of History, awakens mythological reminiscences. The current term 'post-modernity' is rich in such reminiscences. Whenever a myth loses its primeval appeal, the story of a people, a religion, a 'culture', an institution draws to its close. Analogical thinking jumps to the conclusion that, since philosophies of history have lost their appeal, our own, short-lived, Western politico-cultural story has already exhausted all its reserves. Yet this conclusion does not need to be drawn. In so far as they provided modernity with universal stories of intersubjective self-authentication, philosophies of history were the functional equivalents of myths. And yet, as I have pointed out, philosophies of history are unlike myths on several important counts. They can lose their appeal for quite different reasons. Their demise need not to be taken, at least not yet, as a clear indication of our having entered another age identifiable with the prefix 'post'. There are alternative explanations. Myths are experience-resistant, given that fiction and facts merge in them in an undistinguishable unity. Philosophies of history are not. Myths are timeless as long as they live; temporality is their demise. This is not true of philosophies.

By experience-resistance this time I do not mean falsifiability. Philosophical truth is as little open to falsification as mythological truth. Philosophies are not falsified; but one can simply turn away from them. However, personal experience exerts a qualitatively greater influence on the acceptance or the rejection of philosophies than of myths. Commitment to philosophies is always a personal business. Philosophical creeds are not implanted in childhood, and even if they are (as in the case of J. S. Mill) one can shed them and commit oneself to another by mere personal choice. Changing one's vision of the world as a result of personal, historical (non-miraculous) experience pre-supposes the distinction between fact and fiction, whatever that means. One adopts a rational attitude towards philosophies. The constant flux and change of modern philosophical imagination can be attributed mostly to this particular circumstance. The way the so-called 'great narratives' have been emptied out in our lifetime is very much in line with an already traditional rationalistic philosophical attitude. The life experience of my generation was so contrary to the unifying, holistic and truly self-complacent magnificence of the representative philosophies of history that it simply could not bear with them any longer. It would have been highly irrational to stick to the great narratives after their spirit had left the world (to use Hegel's own metaphor). I need to add parenthetically, as a corroboration of what has just been said, that the less dramatic the generational experience, the less dramatic the philosophical change. The greatest drama took place on the European continent.

What does it mean that the spirit that once enlivened great narratives has left the world? It means roughly what it says. A generation with certain historico-personal experiences can no longer subscribe to stories that do not make sense of those experiences. This is why they turn away from philosophies of history of nineteenth-century stock. This is why they can legitimately say that they are untrue.

Yet some caution is warranted here. Though philosophical truth is supposed to be eternal (just like mythological truth), temporality is neither alien nor hostile to philosophy. Depersonification guarantees safe navigation on the ocean of discontinuity. Arguments can be carried from one locus to another like mythological motifs, but they are not just conferred upon any deserving person. Rather, the person who made them first can always be taken to task. Their views can be discussed as theirs, and refuted, criticized, altered or vindicated as such, in any age, by any man or woman of any conviction, even without reference to a whole body of belief. Philosophy of history is gone now, and it seems to have gone for good. But we cannot know, in fact we do not know, whether this is the case. Perhaps one day, in a century or even tomorrow, new stories of world history are going to be told; and men and women will turn towards them because they wil be true (for them).

'The end of X' language, where X can stand for history, the subject, metaphysics, philosophy, man, the West, and much more, is the language of philosophy of history. If we seriously intend to leave philosophy of history behind, at least for the time being, it is advisable also to leave 'the end of X' language behind. For the same reason, post-modernity cannot be interpreted as *post-histoire*, as a new period that comes after modernity and that cancels history as such together with modernity. At any rate, our life experiences do not bear out this proposition. I recommend, therefore, that the term post-modernity be understood as equivalent to the contemporary historical consciousness ·of the modern age. Post-modern is not what follows after the modern age, but what follows after the unfolding of modernity. Once the main categories of modernity have emerged, the historical tempo slows down and the real work on the possibilities begins. These possibilities are open – thus they can be put to better or worse use. This is why statements about future certainties do not appeal to us; nor do reconfirmations of our existence as the very consummation of the whole of human history. Philosophies of history are crutches we no longer need.

IV

When a myth dies because no one believes in it any more, the story, the image that was once a myth, can still remain authentic and true if shifted into another medium. Ormuzd and Ariman, Leda and the swan, are parts of what we term 'culture'. The name of George the dragon-killer has been erased from the list of Catholic saints, but the image of the dragon-killing youth cannot be erased from the world of painting. Philosophy has a status similar to that of art, by which I mean that works of philosophy belong to the realm of 'culture', at least from the time when the Roman age consciously turned back to the Greeks as the source of philosophical wisdom. This is why drawing parallels between the afterlife of myths and that of philosophies seems eminently meaningless. If Aristotle's philosophy survived as philosophy and not as art or religion, the same can be expected from Hegel's. On the other hand, myths and artworks resemble one another more than works of philosophy resemble any of them. One cannot discard a part of a myth and still believe in it. But one can certainly dismiss a few aspects of a philosophy while retaining others. Moreover, this is normal practice in preserving philosophical heritage. There is very little difference in this respect between the philosophical heritage of the remote past and the legacy of the past of the present.

If post-modernity is indeed but the consummation of modernity, the period when the development of the main categories of modernity have been accomplished and the work within them, with them and on them begins, then the great narratives of philosophy of history are nothing but exemplary manifestations of the consciousness of the past of the present. The great narratives of philosophy of history have lost their appeal not because they were too modern, but because they were not modern enough. More precisely, everything that was eminently modern in them will be preserved as well as constantly recycled.

Moses was put in a basket, Hsüan-tsang was tied to a plank and both were left to the mercy of the river and to the secret design of God.

Our age experiences itself as being divided from the past by an ocean. The 'New World' is geographically divided from the Old Continent by the Atlantic Ocean. However, the actual 'new world' is not America but modernity, and the broadest ocean is not the Atlantic but the historical–metahistorical divide between the pre-modern and the modern. Regardless of whether the term 'new world' is meant as a compliment (as in Dvorak's *New World Symphony*) or as a word of abuse (as in Huxley's *Brave New World*), we recognize ourselves in it. We understand ourselves as a new beginning, for better or for worse.

The great historical narratives are modern in so far as they make a strong statement for this new beginning. However, they are not yet prepared to accept the consequences of this new beginning. This is why they are not modern enough. Philosophers of history did not make the simple but meaningful statement: this world is different, it is new. They also felt obliged to prove that the new is the necessary conclusion of everything that happened before in so-called world history, or that it is the final homecoming of the Absolute Idea. The problem with philosophies of history is not foundationalism, but the way they practised it. In grounding modernity philosophico-historically, they have robbed modernity of the foundation of its freedom that the self-same philosophies were so desirous to establish. Miriam, who put the basket with the little Moses on the river Nile, was replaced by 'World History' writ large and by its laws, although the modern world was supposed to be free and undestined. Yet was it indeed meant to be free and undestined?

The way one starts, so one continues. All philosophies of history proceed with the tale until they arrive at the happy ending to which our (modern) age is supposed to be destined. This is a highly unmodern idea. Among others, the novelty of our age consists of the openness of our horizons and the plurality of interpretations of both the present and the past. This openness allows for multiple projects. The multiplicity of projects is promising but at the same time threatening. The point is not that we are ignorant of the end of our story (a feature that we share with every human group and every age), but that we are as yet ignorant as to whether or not our project will be viable in the long run. We have just begun to work in and on modernity. There are formidable problems, both external and internal, to face. Although the project of modernity has spread almost throughout our whole globe, there are high cultures that put up such resistance that they could even reverse the trend. It remains to be seen whether the Khomeni is an exception. And even if the trend is not going to be reversed, we cannot guess whether scriptures will be granted to us in the Seventh Heaven. And we are rightly irritated if someone tells us that he knows all those scriptures in advance.

Many forms of rationalism are modern and viable; so are several kinds of universalism. Yet the universalistic use of rationality is highly problematic. Transcendental statements have universal validity. The truth of such a statement is neither old nor new; it is timeless and thus eternal. The idea that the 'new world' and the new world alone has access to the eternal, that we alone can arrive at the self-consciousness of the eternal, will not appeal to many in the post-modern age, for the simple reason that it is just a weaker version of the philosophies of history. Most of the moderns would rather accept confinement in the prisonhouse of historicity or keep banging at the door of that prisonhouse, than relinquish the freedom of uncertainty. Some of them can remain loyal to universalizing rationalism all the same. Difference is our hallmark.

In spite of all their seemingly antiquated aspects, philosophies of history manifest the past of the present. As manifestations of our own past, they are to some extent also manifestations of our present. To support this statement one needs only to point to the value all moderns share: the value of freedom, both for the philosophers of history and for the rest of us. The only difference is that many post-moderns turn a fairly sceptical eye on the actual status of freedom in the modern age, whereas philosophers of history had, as it were, the happy ending already in sight. The evaluative yardstick has remained unchanged. But, as often happens, the values on which the narratives are built can be identical, whereas the narratives themselves are not only different but also exclusive. This can be the case, but in this particular case it is not.

Stories about history can evoke in the reader authentic experiences that have nothing to do with history. If a great narrative could be perceived as the manifestation of one or another authentic modern experiences, it could be called true, albeit not the Truth of History. Let me mention briefly two such experiences of enormous weight: that of human destiny and that of the divine.

Philosophical narratives are said to have been depersonified. Hegel, who adored Napoleon, did not build his story around the vicissitudes of the self-made-man emperor. Yet one can experience, also interpret, the whole of the Hegelian system as the disguised biography of a mythical self-made man, and not without some justification. Modern men and women are contingent. They are also conscious of their contingency. They are born a bundle of mere possibilities. As I have argued elsewhere,[4] it is only through an existential choice that they can transform their contingency into their destiny. Yet, once they have succeeded in this, their whole life will appear to them retrospectively as a progressive chain of self-development through the dialectical unity of freedom and necessity. This is the process that Hegel actually derived or described. And he also added that what he had done can be done only in a retrospective glance.

The narrative is disappointing only if it is about world history. Read as a universalized biography of modern self-made men or women who succeeded in transforming their contingency into destiny, the same story appears in a totally different and new light. There is no Archimedean point from which one can look back at History. But there are certainly Archimedean points from which people can look back at their own life, from the height of which they can say with well-deserved satisfaction: I have done it, I have become by choice what I am (and what I have always been). Philosophies of histories are true stories about such men and women. Modern human destiny is represented not in one kind of philosophy, but by different kinds of that genre. Not everyone will recognize her or his autobiography in the great narratives of philosophy of history, but some will. And, for them, these stories will be, and remain, true. One does not need to be a Moses or a Hsüan-tsang to embody, or repersonify, world historical narratives.

That men and women use their own imagination to project the images of gods is a statement in which both believers and disbelievers can agree. Traditional images of deities survive traditional societies; so do old myths. Nothing indicates that they may wither. And yet modern life experience and world experience do not leave the image and the concept of the divinity unaffected. True enough, modernity seems to be an age without religious genius or fantasy. One might even add that Europe in general has never excelled in original religious imagination. But one could also argue that religious imagination is not tantamount to mythological imagination, since philosophies (from Plato onwards) have conspicuously contributed to the conception of religious ideas. Maybe the same will be said about modern philosophies a few centuries from now. There is no knowing about this. Yet one can convincingly make a case for the innovative impact of modern philosophies on the present. Three philosophers indicate three different directions: Kierkegaard, Kant and Hegel. History is central for all three of them. Kierkegaard's Christ is the absolute paradox of History; Kant's God is unknown and unknowable, yet also the postulate of freedom and of the best world; Hegel's Absolute Idea is the totality of all that Is in its historical self-development towards itself. The implication is not that modern philosophies of history are but different versions of a theodicy, but that they are *also* reformulations of the human image of that-which-is-higher-than-human, as it appears to those who have just entered the modern age.

I have recounted three stories: that of Moses, that of Hsüan-tsang and that of History writ large. Whatever else they are, they are also stories about crossing the water, crossing the frontier, stories of rebirth. The first two are also spiritual stories, stories of scriptures and revival. They tell us the tale of one particular people, one particular religion, one particular culture. The (modern) spiritual stories of History have so far failed whenever they aimed at something similar. Modernity encompasses many traditions and cultures; it tells the tale of many peoples, many religions, many cultures. These tales are all different and remain so. Without the spice of common spirituality, there is no shared tale. The condition of a common spirituality has already been named; it is called freedom. The political framework for its appearance had already been set: it is called democracy. Yet no spirit has yet filled this framework. As far as modernity is concerned, Moses is still wandering in the desert and Hsüan-tsang has not arrived in India. Curious as we are, we do not know when, how and where we are to arrive, or whether we will arrive at all. What we know for sure is that the next instalment of the story will be written by us.

Notes

1 Sigmund Freud, *Moses and Monotheism*, translated by Katherine Jones, (New York: Vintage, 1955).
2 *The Journey to the West*, translated and edited by Anthony C. Yu (Chicago: University of Chicago Press, 1977).
3 Hans Blumenberg, *Work on Myth* (Cambridge, Mass.: MIT, 1985).
4 Agnes Heller, *Philosophy of Morals* (Oxford: Blackwell, 1990).

Index